AP U.S. HISTORY
CRASH COURSE
TABLE of CONTENTS

PART IV

TEST-TAKING STRATEGIES

ABOUT THIS BOOK

REA's *AP U.S. History Crash Course* is the first book of its kind for the last-minute studier or any AP student who wants a quick refresher on the course. The *Crash Course* is based upon a careful analysis of the new 2015 AP U.S. History Course Description outline and available official AP test questions.

Written by AP U.S. History experts who have studied the content and format of the revised exam, our easy-to-read format gives students a crash course in the major ideas and events in U.S. history. The targeted review chapters offer students a concise way to learn all the important AP material before the test.

Unlike other test preps, REA's *AP U.S. History Crash Course* gives you a review specifically focused on what you really need to study in order to ace the exam. Our review is broken down into specific topics and themes, offering you two ways to study the material—chronologically, or by key themes and facts.

As you've probably heard, the APUSH exam has undergone a major shift that, beginning in 2015, places greater emphasis on reasoning and analysis. So it is with this *Crash Course*, which is designed to give you a critical overview of key events, movements, and individuals contributing to American history.

Our handy format makes this the perfect quick-reference companion.

The *AP U.S. History Crash Course* introduction begins with a discussion of five keys for success and a glossary of 42 AP U.S. History terms you absolutely, positively have to know.

Part Two is composed of review chapters arranged in chronological order. Each chapter presents only the essential information tied to each time period in U.S. History.

Part Three is devoted to key themes in American history, with particular attention focused on African American history, Native American history, and women's history.

Finally, the *Crash Course* concludes with chapters that present strategies for successfully answering all the different question types on the exam—everything from the multiple-choice questions to the document-based essay question.

No matter how or when you prepare for the new AP U.S. History exam, REA's *Crash Course* will show you how to study efficiently and strategically, so you can boost your score.

To check your test readiness for the revised AP U.S. History exam, either before or after studying this *Crash Course*, take REA's **FREE online practice exam**. To access your practice exam, visit the online REA Study Center at *www.rea.com/studycenter* and follow the on-screen instructions. This true-to-format test features automatic scoring, detailed explanations of all answers, and diagnostic score reporting that will help you identify your strengths and weaknesses so you'll be ready on exam day.

Good luck on your AP U.S. History exam!

ABOUT OUR AUTHORS

Greg Feldmeth earned an A.B. degree from Occidental College and master's degrees from the University of California at Berkeley, California State University at Los Angeles, and Columbia University in New York City. He has taught U.S. history for over 40 years, while also offering courses in Contemporary Ethical Issues, Globalization and Human Rights, European History, and World History.

In addition to his teaching, Mr. Feldmeth has served in a number of administrative roles, including Dean of Students, Head of the Upper and Middle Schools, and Interim Head of School. He is currently History Department Co-Chair and Assistant Head of School at the Polytechnic School in Pasadena, California. He also teaches an online course, Genocide and Human Rights, through the Global Online Academy. Mr. Feldmeth has written or edited twelve U.S. history review books for teachers and students.

Larry Krieger earned his B.A. and M.A.T. from the University of North Carolina at Chapel Hill and his M.A. from Wake Forest University. In a career spanning more than 35 years, Mr. Krieger has taught a variety of AP subjects including American History, World History, European History, American Government, and Art History. His popular courses were renowned for their energetic presentations, commitment to scholarship, and helping students achieve high AP exam scores.

ABOUT RESEARCH & EDUCATION ASSOCIATION

Founded in 1959, Research & Education Association (REA) is dedicated to publishing the finest and most effective educational materials—including study guides and test preps—for students in middle school, high school, college, graduate school, and beyond.

Today, REA's wide-ranging catalog is a leading resource for students, teachers, and other professionals. Visit *www.rea.com* to see a complete listing of all our titles.

ACKNOWLEDGMENTS

We would like to thank Pam Weston, Publisher, for setting the quality standards for production integrity and managing the publication to completion; John Paul Cording, Vice President, Technology, for coordinating the design and development of the REA Study Center; Larry B. Kling, Vice President, Editorial, for his overall direction; Diane Goldschmidt, Managing Editor, for coordinating development of this edition; Kathy Caratozzolo of Caragraphics for typesetting this edition; Marianne L'Abbate for copyediting; Ellen Gong for proofreading; and Terry Casey for indexing.

PART I:
INTRODUCTION

FIVE KEYS FOR SUCCESS ON THE AP U.S. HISTORY EXAM

Your AP U.S. History (APUSH) textbook is very thick and contains thousands of names, dates, places, people, and events. Trying to review all of the information in your book from pre-Columbian Indian civilizations until modern times is a daunting task. Where would you begin? What would you emphasize? What information can you safely omit? Must you study everything?

Fortunately, preparing for the APUSH exam does not have to be a nightmare. By studying efficiently and strategically with this book, you can score a 4 or a 5 on the exam. Use the following five keys for success:

1. Understanding the APUSH Scale

The College Board evaluates student performance on all AP exams and assigns a score based on the following five-point scale:

> 5—extremely well qualified
>
> 4—well qualified
>
> 3—qualified
>
> 2—possibly qualified
>
> 1—no recommendation

An AP grade of 3 or higher indicates a student has mastery of course content that would be equivalent to a college-level introductory course. A number of colleges in recent years, however, do not give credit for an AP exam score below 4 or 5. Check with the college you're interested in attending to see what score it requires to receive credit for your AP exam.

2. Understanding the APUSH Concept Outline

APUSH test writers use a detailed concept outline that tells them what they can and cannot ask. This topical outline is freely available. You can access it on the AP U.S. History page of the College Board website. It describes the nine periods of American history that are covered effective with the 2015 exam. As you see in the chart below, some of the periods overlap because historians disagree about how to fix their boundaries.

Period	Date Range	% of AP Exam
1	1491–1607	5%
2	1607–1754	10%
3	1754–1800	12%
4	1800–1848	10%
5	1844–1877	13%
6	1865–1898	13%
7	1890–1945	17%
8	1945–1980	15%
9	1980–Present	5%

Each of the chapters that follow is organized according to this outline and begins with the key concepts of the chronological period.

3. Understanding the Format of the Exam

The revised AP U.S. History exam features four types of questions:

(1) multiple choice

(2) short answer

(3) document-based

(4) long essay

The **multiple-choice** section consists of 55 questions. You will have 55 minutes to answer them. This section is worth 40 percent of your grade. Each question requires analysis of a stimulus, such as an image (painting, cartoon, photograph, etc.), a primary or secondary source, a graph, or a map. You will need an understanding of U.S. history to respond correctly to the question, which will have one correct response and three distractors. The exam has been designed to emphasize your ability to use historical thinking skills rather than merely recalling memorized facts.

Short-answer questions are new to the AP U.S. History exam, beginning with the 2015 exam. You will have 50 minutes to answer four questions. There is no need to include a thesis in your response, but you need to use proper grammatical English and complete sentences. An outline or a bulleted list as your response is not acceptable.

The next type of question is the **document-based question (DBQ).** You will have 55 minutes to answer it. Using the documents provided (which can include graphs, pictures, cartoons, and written materials), you will be asked to analyze and synthesize historical evidence found in the documents. There will be between five and seven documents, and you will need to refer to all, or all but one, of the documents in your response.

For the **long essay question,** the final question type, you will choose one of two comparable prompts to which to respond. You will have 35 minutes to write your response, which should include a strong thesis statement supported by relevant historical evidence.

4. Using Your *Crash Course* to Build a Winning Strategy

This *Crash Course* book is based on a careful analysis of the APUSH *Course Description* topical outline. Chapter 2 contains 42 key terms that you absolutely, positively have to know. Chapters 3–11 provide you with a detailed chronological review of key points derived from the *Course Description*'s topical outline. Chapters 12–22 give you detailed information about key events, themes, and facts. And finally, Chapters 23–26 share test-taking strategies for each section of the APUSH exam.

If you have the time, review the entire book. This is desirable but not mandatory. You can study the chapters in any order. Each chapter provides you with a digest of key information that will be helpful for you to know for the various types of questions. Unlike most review books, the *Crash Course* summaries are not meant to be exhaustive. Instead, they are meant to focus your attention on the most essential material you need to study.

5. Using Additional Materials to Supplement Your *Crash Course*

Your *Crash Course* contains everything you need to know to score a 4 or a 5. You should supplement it, however, with materials provided by the College Board. The College Board's AP Central website contains a wealth of materials, including a free practice exam. In addition, REA's *AP U.S. History All Access*® Book + Web + Mobile study system further enhances your exam preparation by offering a comprehensive review book plus a suite of online assessments (end-of-chapter quizzes, mini-tests, two full-length practice tests, and e-flashcards), all of which are designed to pinpoint your strengths and weaknesses and help focus your study for the exam.

KEY TERMS

I. PERIOD 1: 1491–1607

1. COLUMBIAN EXCHANGE

The Columbian Exchange refers to the exchange of plants, animals, and diseases between Europe and the New World following the discovery of America in 1492.

New World crops such as corn, tomatoes, and potatoes had a dramatic effect on the European diet. At the same time, Old World domesticated animals such as horses, cows, and pigs, had a dramatic effect on life in the New World.

European diseases, such as smallpox, decimated the population of the New World, while venereal diseases were carried back to Europe from the Americas.

II. PERIOD 2: 1607–1754

2. MERCANTILISM

Mercantilism, the economic philosophy guiding Great Britain in the seventeenth and eighteenth centuries, viewed colonies as existing only to benefit the mother country. Like other mercantile powers, Great Britain sought to increase its wealth and power by obtaining large amounts of gold and silver and by establishing a favorable balance of trade with its colonies.

3. HALF-WAY COVENANT

The Puritans established the Half-Way Covenant to ease require-ments for church membership and retain control. The Half-Way Covenant allowed the baptism of the children of baptized, but unconverted, Puritans.

4. ENLIGHTENMENT

The Enlightenment was an eighteenth-century philosophy stress-ing that reason could be used to improve the human condition and that the natural world provided models for human institu-tions.

Enlightenment thinkers such as Thomas Jefferson stressed the idea of natural rights. This idea can clearly be seen in the second para-graph of the Declaration of Independence:

> *"We hold these truths to be self-evident; that all men are created equal; that they are endowed by their Creator with certain inalienable rights; that among these are life, liberty, and the pursuit of happiness."*

5. THE FIRST GREAT AWAKENING

This term refers to a wave of religious revivals that spread across the American colonies during the 1730s and 1740s as the power of the Puritans waned.

 ## PERIOD 3: 1754–1800

6. CONSTITUTIONAL CONVENTION

The 1787 Constitutional Convention sought to correct weakness-es in the Articles of Confederation by creating a strong central government that shared powers with the states.

7. SEPARATION OF POWERS

This term refers to the division of power among the legisla-tive, judicial, and executive branches of government. Alexander

Hamilton defended the principle of separation of powers when he wrote,

> *"There is no liberty if the power of judging be not separated from the legislative and executive powers. . . ."*

8. CHECKS AND BALANCES

This refers to a system in which each branch of government can check the power of the other branches. For example, the president can veto a bill passed by Congress, but Congress can override the president's veto.

9. HAMILTON'S FINANCIAL PLANS

Hamilton sought to create a sound financial footing for the new republic by assuming state debts, creating a national bank, and imposing tariffs to protect home industries.

 PERIOD 4: 1800–1848

10. JUDICIAL REVIEW

The Supreme Court can strike down an act of Congress by declaring it unconstitutional. This principle was established in the case of *Marbury v. Madison.*

11. AMERICAN SYSTEM

Chiefly proposed by Henry Clay, the American System was a set of proposals designed to unify the nation and strengthen its economy by means of protective tariffs, a national bank, and internal improvements such as canals and new roads.

12. REPUBLICAN MOTHERHOOD/CULT OF DOMESTICITY

This idea refers to the idealization of women in their roles as wives and mothers.

The concept of republican motherhood suggested that women would be responsible for raising their children to be virtuous citizens of the new American republic.

13. TRANSCENDENTALISM

Transcendentalism was a philosophical and literary movement of the 1800s that emphasized living a simple life and celebrating the truth found in nature and in personal emotion and imagination. Ralph Waldo Emerson and Henry David Thoreau were the foremost transcendentalist writers.

14. UTOPIAN COMMUNITIES

A number of small, self-sufficient communities developed in the nineteenth century in an attempt to achieve perfection. Perfectionism was the belief that humans can use conscious acts of will to create communities based on cooperation and mutual respect.

Utopian communities such as Brook Farm, New Harmony, and Oneida reflected the blossoming of perfectionist aspirations.

15. THE SECOND GREAT AWAKENING

This refers to a wave of religious enthusiasm that spread across America between 1800 and 1830. Middle-class women played an especially important role in the Second Great Awakening by making Americans aware of the moral issues posed by slavery. The Second Great Awakening also led to reformist zeal for causes such as prison reform and anti-liquor laws.

16. JACKSONIAN DEMOCRACY

This term refers to a set of political beliefs associated with Andrew Jackson and his followers. Jacksonian democracy included respect for the abilities and aspirations of the common man, expansion of white male suffrage, appointment of political supporters to government positions, and opposition to privileged Eastern elites.

17. NULLIFICATION

Nullification is a legal theory that a state in the United States has the right to nullify (invalidate) any federal law that the state deems unconstitutional. The concept was first introduced by Thomas Jefferson and James Madison in the Virginia and Kentucky Resolutions in 1798.

John C. Calhoun was also a proponent of the doctrine of nullification. Inspired by his leadership, a convention in South Carolina declared the tariffs of both 1828 and 1832 unenforceable in that state.

V. PERIOD 5: 1844–1877

18. MANIFEST DESTINY

This refers to the nineteenth-century belief that the United States had an obligation to expand westward to the Pacific Ocean.

19. POPULAR SOVEREIGNTY

Popular sovereignty is the principle that the settlers of a given territory have the sole right to decide whether slavery will be permitted there.

Popular sovereignty led to a divisive debate over the expansion of slavery into the territories. The first great test of popular sovereignty occurred in Kansas following passage of the Kansas-Nebraska Act.

20. RECONSTRUCTION

Implemented by Congress, Reconstruction focused on reorganizing the governments of the Southern states after the Civil War and allowing them to reenter the Union.

VI. PERIOD 6: 1865–1898

21. SOCIAL GOSPEL

The Social Gospel refers to a nineteenth-century reform movement based on the belief that Christians have a responsibility to confront social problems such as poverty actively. Led by Christian ministers, advocates of the Social Gospel argued that real social change would result from dedication to both religious practice and social reform.

22. GOSPEL OF WEALTH

This was the belief that the wealthy were the guardians of society and, as such, had a duty to serve and lead society in humane ways. Andrew Carnegie was the foremost advocate of the Gospel of Wealth.

23. SOCIAL DARWINISM

This refers to the belief that in society, as in nature, a natural evolutionary process occurs, with the fittest surviving. Wealthy business and industrial leaders such as John D. Rockefeller used Social Darwinism to justify their success. He wrote:

> *"The growth of a large business corporation is merely survival of the fittest . . . the American Beauty rose can be produced in the splendor and fragrance which brings cheer to its beholder only by sacrificing the early buds which grow up around it. This is not an evil tendency in business. It is merely the working out of a law of nature and a law of God."*

24. FRONTIER THESIS

This term refers to the argument by historian Frederick Jackson Turner that the frontier experience helped make American society more democratic and shaped American values. Turner especially emphasized the importance of cheap, unsettled land and the inspirational power of the frontier to spur democracy. Here is an illustrative quote:

> *"From the beginning of the settlement of America, the frontier regions have exercised a steady influence toward democracy . . . American democracy is fundamentally the outcome of the experience of the American people in dealing with the West . . . ."*

25. NEW IMMIGRANTS

This term refers to the massive wave of immigrants who came to the United States between 1880 and 1924.

The Old Immigrants came primarily from England, Germany, and Scandinavia. The New Immigrants came primarily from small farms and villages in Southern and Eastern Europe.

26. NATIVISM

Nativists favored the interests of native-born people over the interests of immigrants.

The Know-Nothings of the 1840s were the first nativist political party, but nativism grew stronger with the arrival of large new immigrant groups. Nativists usually directed their greatest hostility toward Irish and German Catholic immigrants.

27. VERTICAL AND HORIZONTAL INTEGRATION

Vertical integration occurs when a company controls both the production and distribution of its product. For example, Andrew Carnegie used vertical integration to gain control over the U.S. steel industry.

Horizontal integration occurs when one company gains control over other companies that produce the same product. For example, John D. Rockefeller used horizontal integration in the oil industry.

 PERIOD 7: 1890–1945

28. POPULISM

This term refers to the mainly agrarian movement developed in the 1890s that supported the unlimited coinage of silver, government ownership of the railroads, and other policies that favored farmers and the working class.

29. PROGRESSIVISM

Progressivism sought to use government to help create a more just society. They fought against impure foods, child labor, corruption, and trusts. Theodore Roosevelt and Woodrow Wilson were prominent Progressive presidents.

30. MUCKRAKERS

These were early twentieth-century journalists who exposed illegal business practices, social injustices, and corrupt urban political bosses. Leading muckrakers included Upton Sinclair, Jacob Riis, and Ida Tarbell.

31. ROARING TWENTIES

This refers to the period of social unrest and tension that occurred in the 1920s with immigration restrictions, the rise of fundamentalism, and changing sexual values.

32. PROHIBITION

From 1919 to 1933, it was illegal to buy, sell, or transport alcohol throughout the United States. It led to a rise in organized crime and defiance of the law until the constitutional amendment establishing prohibition of alcohol was repealed.

33. ISOLATIONISM

Isolationism was a U.S. foreign policy calling for Americans to avoid entangling political alliances following World War I. During the 1930s, isolationists drew support from ideas expressed in Washington's Farewell Address. The Neutrality Acts of the 1930s were expressions of a commitment to isolationism.

 PERIOD 8: 1945–1980

34. CONTAINMENT

Containment defined U.S. foreign policy during the Cold War and was designed to contain or block the spread of communism.

George F. Kennan was an American diplomat and specialist on the Soviet Union who advocated, in what has become known as the Long Telegram, that the United States focus its foreign policy on containing the spread of Soviet influence.

35. McCARTHYISM

This term refers to the public accusations of disloyalty without sufficient evidence, which increased following World War II.

Senator Joseph R. McCarthy played on the fears of Americans by claiming that communists had infiltrated the U.S. State Department and other federal agencies. Senator McCarthy's accusations helped create a climate of paranoia as Americans became preoccupied with the perceived threat posed by alleged communists working in the United States.

36. DOMINO THEORY

This theory refers to the belief that, if one country falls to communism, its neighbors will also be infected and fall to communism. For example, the fall of South Vietnam would lead to the loss of all of Southeast Asia.

The following statement by a U.S. secretary of state illustrates the domino theory:

> *"If Indo-China were to fall and if its fall led to the loss of all of Southeast Asia, then the United States might eventually be forced back to Hawaii, as it was before the Second World War."*

37. MASSIVE RETALIATION

A military doctrine developed during the Cold War that asserted that, in the event of an attack by the Soviet Union or any other hostile power, the United States would retaliate with massive force, including nuclear weapons.

The threat of massive retaliation was viewed as a deterrent to a preemptive strike launched by an enemy of the United States.

38. BLACK POWER

The Black Power movement of the 1960s advocated that African Americans establish control of their political and economic lives. Key advocates of Black Power included Malcolm X, Stokely Carmichael, and Huey Newton.

39. WATERGATE

This term refers to a series of political scandals and cover-ups that resulted in Richard Nixon being the only president to resign from office; he did so in 1974.

40. DÉTENTE

The term refers to the relaxation of tensions between the United States and the Soviet Union; it was introduced by Secretary of State Henry Kissinger and President Richard Nixon. Examples of détente include the Strategic Arms Limitation Talks (SALT), expanded trade with the Soviet Union, and President Nixon's trips to China and Russia.

IX. PERIOD 9: 1980–PRESENT

41. REAGANOMICS

The term *Reaganomics* refers to the economic policies of President Ronald Reagan; it is also called supply-side economics. President Reagan hoped to promote growth and investment by deregulating business, reducing corporate tax rates, and lowering federal tax rates for upper- and middle-income Americans.

42. AFFIRMATIVE ACTION

This refers to attempts to open access to education and employment for members of groups that experienced discrimination (based on race, ethnicity, sex, etc.). Affirmative action laws sometimes imposed quotas for college admissions and hiring to address past injustices or current underrepresentation.

PART II:
CONTENT
Review

PERIOD 1
—— 1491*–1607

Key Concepts†

Concept 1: Before the arrival of Europeans, native populations in North America developed a wide variety of social, political, and economic structures based in part on interactions with the environment and each other.

Concept 2: European overseas expansion resulted in the Columbian Exchange, a series of interactions and adaptations among societies on both sides of the Atlantic.

Concept 3: Contacts among American Indians, Africans, and Europeans challenged the worldviews of each group.

I. THE FIRST AMERICANS

A. ARRIVAL AND DISPERSAL

1. The earliest North American residents crossed a land bridge between Siberia and Alaska between 15,000 and 30,000 years ago.

2. Following large game animals, these Asian immigrants gradually spread through North and South America, reaching the tip of South America by 9,000 BCE.

B. CULTURAL DIVERSITY

1. The Incas, Mayas, and Aztecs were the most advanced of the 2,000 separate cultures that developed in the New World.

---

* The College Board's course framework is built around the study of central themes and key concepts across nine chronological periods. These periods span pre-Columbian contacts in North America (symbolized by the year 1491) to the present.

† © 2014 The College Board.

2. The Anasazi, in what is now Arizona and New Mexico, built cliff-dwellings, roads, and canals.

3. Mississippi Valley tribes developed a farming culture around 800 BCE. They built large earthen pyramids and established trading networks throughout much of North America.

4. Eastern Woodland Indians occupied the land east of the Mississippi River in small, self-governing clans.

5. Plains Indians developed a nomadic lifestyle, following buffalo herds across the American Plains.

C. CONTACT WITH EUROPEANS—THE COLUMBIAN EXCHANGE

1. The arrival of the Europeans greatly affected Indian cultures.

2. Massive epidemics in the Caribbean and Mexico occurred as native populations contracted European diseases.

3. Tribes along the Atlantic Coast and the Ohio River Valley were pressured to adapt to white settlers and traders, and became dependent on fur trading.

4. Europeans attempted to civilize Indians and have them accept Christianity.

5. Plains Indians used guns and horses to expand their range and attack enemy tribes.

D. SIMILARITIES AND DIFFERENCES BETWEEN INDIANS AND EUROPEAN SETTLERS

1. Similarities included the following:

   ▶ Both lived in village communities.

   ▶ Both shared a strong sense of spirituality.

   ▶ Both divided labor by gender.

2. Differences included the following:

   ▶ Indians did not share the European concept of private property.

   ▶ Indian children were often part of their mother's clan because many cultures were matrilineal.

PERIOD 2
—— 1607–1754

Key Concepts†

> **Concept 1:** Differences in imperial goals, cultures, and the North American environments led Europeans to develop diverse patterns of colonization.
>
> **Concept 2:** European colonization efforts in North America stimulated intercultural contact and intensified conflict among the various groups of colonists and native peoples.
>
> **Concept 3:** The increasing political, economic, and cultural exchanges with the Atlantic World had a profound impact on the development of colonial societies in North America.

I. THE PLANTATION COLONIES

A. THE VIRGINIA COMPANY

1. Established as a joint-stock company in 1607.

2. Its primary goal was profit making for stockholders.

3. Religious motivation was much less important to its founding compared to Massachusetts Bay, Maryland, Pennsylvania, and Rhode Island.

4. The population was mostly male, and these settlers were interested in getting rich quick, not establishing a permanent colony.

---

† © 2014 The College Board.

B. TOBACCO

1. Tobacco cultivation made the British colonies in the Chesapeake region economically viable as European demand for tobacco increased.

2. By the mid-1700s, tobacco was the most valuable cash crop produced in the Southern colonies.

 ## II. THE PLANTATION COLONIES AND THE GROWTH OF SLAVERY

A. FROM SERVITUDE TO SLAVERY IN THE CHESAPEAKE REGION, 1607–1690

1. Indentured servants played a key role in the growth of the tobacco plantation system in the Chesapeake. They were the chief source of agricultural labor in these colonies before 1675. Servants worked for a period of time in exchange for their passage to America.

2. Planters in Virginia and Maryland used the headright system to encourage the importation of indentured servants— whoever paid the passage of a laborer received the right to purchase 50 acres of land.

3. The number of slaves increased dramatically in the last quarter of the seventeenth century because they were a more reliable source of permanent labor.

4. Slave labor in colonial Virginia spread rapidly in the late seventeenth century, and blacks displaced white indentured servants in the tobacco fields.

5. Legal restrictions on slaves developed; these restrictions limited their freedoms and rights.

B. BACON'S REBELLION, 1676

1. Bacon's Rebellion in Virginia exposed tensions between the former indentured servants, who were poor, and the gentry (the genteel class of planters), who were rich.

2. As planters became more suspicious of their former indentured servants, they turned to slaves as more reliable sources of labor.

3. Bacon's Rebellion failed, but it pointed to the danger of antagonism between the wealthy class and poor farmers.

C. GROWTH OF PLANTATION ECONOMIES AND SLAVE SOCIETIES, 1690–1754

1. Slavery developed and spread because the cultivation of tobacco demanded inexpensive labor.

2. Slavery was legally established in all thirteen colonies by the early 1700s.

3. Although enslaved, Africans sought to retain cultural practices brought from Africa.

4. Rice was the most important crop grown in South Carolina during the mid-eighteenth century.

5. The Stono Rebellion (1739) was one of the earliest known acts of rebellion against slavery in the United States. Organized and led by slaves living south of Charleston, South Carolina, participants tried to flee to Spanish Florida, where they hoped to gain their freedom.

III. THE SEPARATISTS AND THE PURITANS

A. KEY FACTS

1. Separatists (Pilgrims) arrived in Plymouth in 1620, declaring the principle of self-government with the Mayflower Compact.

2. The Puritans usually came to New England in family groups. They wanted to escape political repression, religious restrictions, and an economic recession.

3. Led by John Winthrop, they sought to establish a model of a united Christian community. Because of this desire for unity, they harshly suppressed dissenting voices.

4. The Puritans typically lived in small villages surrounded by farmland.

5. Puritan leaders held both political and religious authority.

6. The Puritans believed strongly in the value of education for both boys and girls and the necessity for a trained and educated ministry. They founded Harvard College and Yale College to ensure an adequate supply of ministers.

B. "A CITY UPON A HILL"

1. John Winthrop called on the Puritans to build a model society, which he referred to as "a city upon a hill."

2. The Puritans had a powerful sense of mission—to build an ideal Christian community.

3. The Puritans had a strict code of moral conduct for all community members and enforced conformity.

4. Here is the quote from Winthrop's famous sermon, in which he defined the purpose of the Puritan colony:

   "For we must consider that we shall be as a city upon a hill. The eyes of all people are upon us. So that if we shall deal falsely with our God in this work we have undertaken, and so cause Him to withdraw His present help from us, we shall be made a story and a by-word through the world."

C. THE PURITANS AND RELIGIOUS FREEDOM

1. The Puritans immigrated to America for religious freedom yet did not tolerate religious dissent or diversity.

2. Not all Puritans shared Winthrop's vision—both Anne Hutchinson and Roger Williams were expelled for challenging the Puritan authorities.

D. ANNE HUTCHINSON

1. She struggled with the Massachusetts Bay authorities over religious doctrine and gender roles, challenging the teachings and authority of the male clerical hierarchy and claiming to receive revelations directly from God.

2. She was banished to Rhode Island and later moved to New York, where she and all but one of her younger children were killed by Indians.

Few Americans can identify Anne Hutchinson. She is most frequently remembered by New York motorists driving on the Hutchinson River Parkway and by tourists who admire her statue in front of the Boston statehouse. Hutchinson is a noteworthy example of the strong tradition of American dissenters who challenged authority, whether political or religious.

E. ROGER WILLIAMS

1. Expelled by the Massachusetts Bay authorities, Roger Williams founded the colony of Rhode Island.

2. He advanced the cause of religious toleration and freedom of thought.

3. He believed that the state was an improper and ineffectual agent in matters of spiritual concerns and helped establish the tradition of separation of church and state.

F. THE HALF-WAY COVENANT

1. As time passed, the Puritans' religious zeal began to diminish and church membership declined.

2. The Half-Way Covenant eased requirements for church membership by allowing the baptism of the children of baptized, but unconverted, Puritans.

G. SALEM WITCHCRAFT CRISIS

1. An anti-witchcraft hysteria developed in Salem, Massachusetts, in 1692.

2. Community members accused others, mostly women, of being witches, which resulted in trials for dozens and the execution of twenty people.

3. Anti-Puritan sentiments developed following the trials and executions, leading to a weakening of Puritan authority.

CONTENT REVIEW

H. THE FIRST GREAT AWAKENING

1. Key points to remember about the First Great Awakening:

   ▶ It took the form of a wave of religious revivals that began in New England in the 1730s.

   ▶ The wave soon swept across all the colonies during the 1740s, bringing a renewed sense of piety and growth in Protestant denominations, particularly Baptists, Presbyterians, and Methodists.

2. A key consequence was that New Light ministers advocated an emotional approach to religious practice; this weakened the authority of traditional Old Light ministers and established churches.

3. New Light ministers did the following:

   ▶ Promoted the growth of New Light institutions of higher learning, such as Princeton, Brown, and Dartmouth.

   ▶ Sparked a renewed missionary spirit that led to the conversion of many slaves.

   ▶ Led to a greater appreciation for the emotional experiences of faith.

   ▶ Added to the growing popularity of itinerant ministers.

   ▶ Increased the number of women in church congregations. Women became the majority in many church congregations.

   ▶ Led to divisions within both the Presbyterian and Congregational churches, resulting in growing religious diversity.

   ▶ Encouraged challenges to religious authority that led to challenges to political authority during the 1760s and 1770s.

Although the APUSH exam has changed, be aware that the First Great Awakening was a popular essay topic on recent APUSH exams. It may still be. Be sure to pay special attention to reviewing the **results** of the First Great Awakening.

IV. PENNSYLVANIA AND THE QUAKERS

A. PENNSYLVANIA

1. Founded by William Penn.

2. Penn created an unusually liberal and tolerant colony, including a representative assembly elected by the landowners.

3. Pennsylvania granted freedom of religion to all citizens and did not have a state-supported church.

B. QUAKERS

1. Quakers were pacifists who refused to bear arms.

2. Quakers advocated freedom of worship and accepted a greater role for women in church services.

3. Quakers opposed slavery and were among America's first abolitionists.

4. Quakers claimed direct revelation from God for all members and opposed a formal clergy.

V. COLONIAL SOCIETY IN THE EIGHTEENTH CENTURY

A. KEY FEATURES

1. Northern merchants and Southern planters amassed great wealth. Despite this, colonial society did not have a hereditary aristocracy.

2. The number of non-English settlers continued to increase. For example, Scotch-Irish and German immigrants moved into Appalachia as the Native Americans were defeated.

3. The thirteen colonies featured religious pluralism. As a result, there was no single dominant Protestant denomination.

4. Slavery was generally accepted as a labor system when the indentured servant system declined. The institution was legally established in all the colonies.

5. Functioning primarily as mercantile centers, colonial cities collected agricultural goods and distributed imported manufactured goods. Most colonial cities were ports that maintained close economic and cultural ties with England.

B. MERCANTILISM AND THE NAVIGATION ACTS

1. Mercantilism was England's dominant economic philosophy during the seventeenth and eighteenth centuries.

2. The goal of mercantilism was for England to have a favorable balance of trade. To achieve this goal, the colonies were expected to export their raw materials and import England's finished goods.

3. Mercantilism was designed to protect English industry and promote England's prosperity. It measured wealth by the money in the English treasury.

4. The Navigation Acts were a significant part of British mercantilism. They listed colonial products that could be shipped only to England.

5. The mercantilist system led to the subordination of the colonial economy to that of the mother country.

6. The North American colonies took advantage of Great Britain's policy of salutary neglect to work out trade agreements with other countries so they could acquire needed products. While legally restrictive of trade, the Navigation Acts were loosely enforced.

C. WOMEN IN COLONIAL AMERICA

1. During the colonial period, a woman usually lost control of her property when she married.

2. A married woman had no separate legal identity apart from her husband; single women and widows had the right to own property.

3. While colonial women had fewer rights than women today, they had more rights than any contemporary society in Europe or elsewhere.

D. REPUBLICAN GOVERNMENT/REPUBLICANISM

1. Republicanism is the belief that government should be based on the consent of the governed. British philosopher John Locke developed this concept during the Glorious Revolution of the seventeenth century.

2. Republicanism inspired eighteenth-century American revolutionaries.

3. Key principles of republicanism included the following:

   ▸ Sovereignty comes from the people. Representation should therefore be apportioned based on population.

   ▸ A republic is preferable to a monarchy because it would establish a small, limited government that is responsible to the people.

   ▸ Widespread ownership of property is the bulwark of republican government.

   ▸ Standing armies are dangerous and should be avoided.

   ▸ Agrarian life is both desirable and virtuous.

   ▸ Citizens have the right and perhaps the responsibility to rebel if a sovereign does not honor their rights.

E. ENLIGHTENMENT THINKING

1. Elements of European Enlightenment thinking began influencing prominent Americans.

2. The Enlightenment sought to apply scientific principles to politics and religion, and valued literature and visual and performing arts as important disciplines in colleges, such as King's College (now Columbia University) and the College of Philadelphia (now the University of Pennsylvania).

3. Enlightenment thinkers such as Ben Franklin, Thomas Jefferson, and John Adams began publicly discussing the prospect of political independence from England.

F. COLONIAL LITERATURE

1. Anne Bradstreet (1612–1672) was the first notable American poet and the first woman to be published in colonial America.

2. Phillis Wheatley (1753–1784) was the first published African American poet. Her writing helped create the genre of African American literature.

PERIOD 3
1754–1800

Key Concepts[†]

Concept 1: Britain's victory over France in the imperial struggle for North America led to new conflicts among the British government, the North American colonists, and the American Indians, culminating in the creation of a new nation, the United States.

Concept 2: In the late eighteenth century, new experiments with democratic ideas and republican forms of government, as well as other new religious, economic, and cultural ideas, challenged traditional imperial systems in the Atlantic world.

Concept 3: Migration within North America, cooperative interaction, and competition for resources raised questions about boundaries and policies; intensified conflicts among peoples and nations; and led to contests over the creation of a multiethnic, multiracial national identity.

I. THE ROAD TO REVOLUTION

A. THE FRENCH AND INDIAN WAR, 1754–1763

1. As a result of the British victory in the French and Indian War, France relinquished its North American empire. England now dominated most of the land east of the Mississippi, as well as parts of Canada.

2. The French and Indian War was a pivotal point in America's relationship with Great Britain because it resulted in the British imposing revenue taxes on the colonies and abandoning the policy of benign neglect.

[†] © 2014 The College Board.

B. THE PROCLAMATION OF 1763

1. The Proclamation of 1763 forbade British colonists from crossing a boundary line along the crest of the Appalachian Mountains.

2. The primary purpose of the Proclamation of 1763 was to avoid conflict between the trans-Appalachian Indians and British colonists seeking inexpensive land.

3. It resulted in resentment among colonists, particularly the independent-minded residents of the backcountry.

C. THE STAMP ACT, 1765

1. The act's primary purpose was to raise revenue to support British troops stationed in America. It represented a shift in the purpose of taxation by Parliament, which before had been to regulate trade rather than to generate revenue.

2. The issues raised by the Stamp Act were the following:

   ▶ Does Parliament have the right to tax the colonies?

   ▶ Can members of Parliament truly reflect colonial interests?

3. A debate was provoked over the issue; it led to the rallying cry: "No taxation without representation."

4. The act was important for the following reasons:

   ▶ The colonists demonstrated their willingness to use economic boycotts and violence rather than legal means to frustrate British policy.

   ▶ The British maintained that the colonies had no right to independence from parliamentary authority and were effectively represented in Parliament.

   ▶ Patriot leaders claimed that the act denied them their British birthrights.

   ▶ Many colonists believed they were entitled to all the rights and privileges of British subjects.

5. The act was repealed because the colonists boycotted British exports.

D. THE COERCIVE ACTS, 1774

1. The Coercive Acts were Parliament's angry response to the Boston Tea Party, in which colonists destroyed chests of tea rather than pay a British tax.

2. The Acts were designed to punish Massachusetts in general and Boston in particular. Massachusetts lost many of its chartered rights, and the Port of Boston was closed until the damages caused by the Tea Party participants were paid.

E. *COMMON SENSE*, 1776

1. *Common Sense*, a political pamphlet written by Thomas Paine, was a strongly worded call for independence from Great Britain.

2. Paine opposed the monarchy (he called King George a Pharaoh!) and strongly favored republican government.

3. He offered a vigorous defense of republican principles.

4. Paine's words helped overcome the loyalty many still felt for the monarchy and the mother country.

5. In *Common Sense*, Paine used biblical analogies and natural world references to illustrate his arguments.

F. THE DECLARATION OF INDEPENDENCE, 1776

1. The authors of the Declaration of Independence used the philosophy of natural rights, derived from the writings of John Locke, including the right of an oppressed people to alter or abolish an unjust government.

2. The authors appealed to the sympathies of the English people and accused George III of tyranny.

3. They declared that the colonies were now independent states.

II. THE REVOLUTIONARY WAR, 1775–1781

A. REASONS COLONISTS SUPPORTED THE WAR

1. The colonists believed that George III was a tyrant.

2. They believed that Parliament wanted to control the internal affairs of the colonies without the consent of the colonists, an abuse of their rights as British subjects.

3. They were convinced that British ministers and other government officials had a corrupting influence on the colonists.

4. The colonists wanted greater political participation in policies affecting the colonies.

5. They resented the quartering of British troops in colonial homes.

6. The colonists wanted to preserve their local autonomy and way of life from British interference.

B. THE FRENCH-AMERICAN ALLIANCE AND THE KEY BATTLE OF SARATOGA, 1777

1. The Battle of Saratoga was a turning point in the American Revolution because it convinced the French government to declare war on Great Britain and openly aid the American cause.

2. French military and financial assistance played a decisive role in enabling America to win the Revolutionary War.

3. French leaders were not motivated by a commitment to republican ideals. Their primary motivation was to weaken the British Empire.

4. The French-American alliance influenced the British to offer generous peace terms in the Treaty of Paris.

APUSH test writers rarely ask questions about battles, but the Battle of Saratoga is an exception. Although you are not expected to know the military tactics or commanders, be sure you know the consequences and importance of this pivotal battle.

C. THE TREATY OF PARIS, 1783

1. The treaty established America's new boundaries. The United States now stretched west to the Mississippi, north to the Great Lakes, and south to Spanish Florida.

2. America agreed that loyalists would not be further persecuted.

3. Great Britain agreed to give up fur-trading posts in the West.

 III. **FROM THE ARTICLES OF CONFEDERATION TO THE CONSTITUTION**

A. THE ARTICLES OF CONFEDERATION

1. The writers of the Articles of Confederation were cautious about giving the new government powers they had just denied Parliament.

2. Weaknesses in the Articles included the following:

   ▶ A lack of authority to tax or to exercise authority directly over the states, including the inability to regulate interstate trade, which created tensions between states.

   ▶ A lack of a central authority, including no executive or judicial branches.

3. The most important accomplishments of the Articles of Confederation were the Land Ordinance of 1785 and the Northwest Ordinance of 1787. These two acts:

   ▶ Established the pattern of surveying new townships in the federal territories.

▸ Provided for the orderly creation of territorial governments and new states. Ohio was the first state admitted to the Union from the Northwest Territory.

▸ Excluded slavery north of the Ohio River.

▸ Supported public education.

B. SHAYS'S REBELLION, 1786

1. Sparked by the economic frustrations of Massachusetts farmers, who were losing their farms because they could not pay debts in hard currency. The rebellion was short-lived but pointed to weaknesses in the government under the Articles of Confederation.

2. The leaders of Shays's Rebellion sought these changes:

   ▸ An end to farm foreclosures

   ▸ An end to imprisonment for debt

   ▸ Relief from oppressively high taxation

   ▸ Increased circulation of paper money

3. The leaders of Shays's Rebellion did *not* attempt to overthrow the government of Massachusetts.

4. Shays's Rebellion helped convince key leaders, including Alexander Hamilton and James Madison, that the Articles of Confederation were too weak and that the United States needed a stronger central government.

C. THE FEDERAL CONSTITUTION

1. The Constitution was the result of a series of compromises at the Constitutional Convention that created a government acceptable to large and small states, as well as to free and slave states.

2. The following provisions were in the Constitution as submitted to the states for ratification in 1787:

   ▸ The separation of powers, which organized the national government into three branches

- The authority of Congress to declare war

- A guarantee of the legality of slavery

- The creation of an electoral college to safeguard the presidency from direct popular election

- A provision for impeachment of the president

- A provision for ratifying the Constitution (nine out of thirteen states required)

- Federalism—sharing power between state governments and the federal government

- A bicameral legislature, as created by the Great Compromise, with population determining the allotment of representatives in the House of Representatives and each state receiving two votes in the Senate

- Listing the powers of Congress

- The Three-Fifths Compromise—slaves counted as three-fifths of a person for purposes of both representation and taxation.

3. The following provisions were *not* in the Constitution as submitted to the states in 1787:

- A two-term limit for presidents

- Universal male suffrage

- A presidential cabinet

- The direct election of senators by the people

- Guarantees of freedom of speech and of the press (added in the Bill of Rights)

- The right to a speedy and public trial (added in the Bill of Rights)

- The idea of political parties. The framers opposed political parties. They believed that political parties promoted selfish interests, caused divisions, and thus threatened the existence of republican government.

Remember, the Bill of Rights was not part of the Constitution as ratified in 1788. It was added in 1791. Guarantees of freedom of speech and the press were not part of the Constitution when it was ratified. Many of the rights we now consider constitutional protections were not in the original Constitution. Be clear in your answers about what was and was not in the original Constitution.

D. THE FEDERALIST PAPERS, 1787

1. Alexander Hamilton and James Madison wrote most of the Federalist Papers (sometimes known as The Federalist) in support of ratification of the 1787 Constitution.

2. Madison and Hamilton asserted that a large republic offered the best protection of minority rights. "In an expanding Republic," wrote Madison, "so many different groups and viewpoints would be included in the Congress that tyranny by the majority would be impossible."

E. ANTI-FEDERALISTS

1. Those opposed to the Constitution's establishment of a powerful central government worried that it would become tyrannical.

2. Opponents of federalism (anti-federalists) did the following:

   ‣ Drew support primarily from rural areas

   ‣ Argued that the president would have too much power

   ‣ Feared that Congress would levy heavy taxes

   ‣ Feared that the government would raise a standing army

   ‣ Believed that the new national government would overwhelm the states

   ‣ Argued that individual rights needed to be protected

IV. THE FEDERALIST ERA

A. WASHINGTON AND THE FEDERALISTS TAKE COMMAND

1. George Washington ran unopposed in 1789 and was re-elected easily in 1792.

2. His cabinet featured many veterans of the struggle for independence and two who had very different views of the future of the Republic: Thomas Jefferson and Alexander Hamilton.

B. JEFFERSON'S VIEWS

1. Jefferson believed the greatest threat to freedom was tyrannical government. Thus, government needed to be limited in its powers and completely responsive to the needs and desires of the people.

2. His supporters, who were called Democratic-Republicans, feared that the spirit of democracy that had spurred the Revolution would be lost with a strong central government.

3. The Democratic-Republicans supported the French Revolution and advocated war with England and Spain.

C. HAMILTON'S VIEWS

1. Hamilton greatly feared mobs (such as Shays's Rebellion) and therefore believed that sovereignty must rest with a strong central government that was insensitive to the popular will and remote from the people's emotional uprisings.

2. The aim of Hamilton's economic policies was to:

   ▶ Promote economic growth and home industries

   ▶ Strengthen the new nation's finances

   ▶ Give financial interests such as Eastern merchants a stake in the new government ("A national debt," Hamilton observed, "if it is not excessive will be to us a national blessing. It will be a powerful cement to our union.")

CONTENT REVIEW

3. The Federalists viewed Great Britain as a protector of property rights against French anarchy.

D. HAMILTON'S ECONOMIC PROPOSALS

1. Hamilton proposed to:

   ▶ Establish a national bank

   ▶ Adopt a protective tariff to raise revenue

   ▶ Fund the national debt

   ▶ Assume state debts incurred during the Revolutionary War

   ▶ Tax distilled liquor to raise revenue

   ▶ Expand domestic manufacturing

   ▶ Subsidize domestic manufacturers (Note: Congress rejected this proposal.)

E. CONTROVERSY WITH JEFFERSON

1. Hamilton favored a "loose" interpretation of the Constitution. He used the implied powers of the Necessary and Proper Clause to justify his proposals. Hamilton believed that what the Constitution does not forbid, it permits.

2. Jefferson favored a "strict" interpretation of the Constitution. He believed that what the Constitution does not permit, it forbids.

Test Tip

Hamilton's financial plans and his conflicting vision with Jefferson about the best course for the United States is a frequent AP topic from the Federalist Era and important to understand fully.

V. WASHINGTON'S FAREWELL ADDRESS

A. THE WARNINGS

1. Washington warned Americans against the dangers of factions (parties) within the nation.

2. He also warned about the dangers of entangling alliances with other nations. Washington advised:

   "The great rule of conduct for us in regard to foreign nations, is in extending our commercial relations, to have with them as little political connection as possible. So far as we have already formed engagements, let them be fulfilled with perfect good faith. Here let us stop."

B. IMPACT ON AMERICAN FOREIGN POLICY

1. On many occasions, U.S. political leaders have disregarded Washington's advice and taken an active role in world affairs.

2. President Wilson's opponents would quote Washington to justify their opposition to the League of Nations.

3. During the 1930s, isolationists would use Washington's Farewell Address to justify their support of the Neutrality Acts.

 ## VI. JOHN ADAMS'S ADMINISTRATION

A. ADAMS EXPERIENCED TWO DIFFICULT ENCOUNTERS WITH FRANCE

1. In the XYZ Affair, French agents demanded bribes before negotiating with American representatives, which led some to call for war with France.

2. A naval war with France raged for two years, with ninety French ships captured before France agreed to American terms in the Convention of 1800.

B. **THE FEDERALISTS PASSED THE ALIEN AND SEDITION ACTS IN ATTEMPTS TO MAKE IT MORE DIFFICULT TO BECOME A CITIZEN AND TO LIMIT CRITICISM OF THE GOVERNMENT AND PRESIDENT**

1. Jefferson and Madison responded by writing the Kentucky and Virginia Resolutions, which presented their view of nullification—a state could disregard a federal law if it decided that the law was unconstitutional.

2. Adams's popularity declined and Jefferson won the election of 1800, ending Federalist control of the executive branch.

On previous APUSH exams, John Adams appeared only in conjunction with the quasi-war with France and the Alien and Sedition Acts. However, the importance of the Alien and Sedition Acts cannot be overstated. The Federalist Party (which controlled all three branches of government in 1798) clearly overreached its constitutional authority and was therefore ousted by Jefferson's party in the election of 1800. The Federalist Party never fully recovered and ceased to exist on a national level by 1820.

PERIOD 4
1800–1848

Key Concepts†

Concept 1: The United States developed the world's first modern mass democracy and celebrated a new national culture. Americans sought to define the nation's democratic ideals and to reform its institutions to match them.

Concept 2: Developments in technology, agriculture, and commerce precipitated profound changes in U.S. settlement patterns, regional identities, gender and family relations, political power, and distribution of consumer goods.

Concept 3: The United States' interest in increasing foreign trade, expanding its national borders, and isolating itself from European conflicts shaped the nation's foreign policy and spurred government and private initiatives.

I. THE ERA OF THOMAS JEFFERSON

A. THE "REVOLUTION OF 1800"

1. The victory of Jefferson and the Democratic-Republicans marked the end of what has been called the Federalist Era.

2. The election of 1800 is called a "revolution" because the incumbent party gave up power peacefully after losing an election.

B. KEY TENETS OF JEFFERSONIAN DEMOCRACY

1. The yeoman farmer best exemplifies virtue and independence from the corrupting influences of cities, bankers, financiers, and industrialists.

---

2. The federal government must not violate states' rights, which was proclaimed in the Kentucky and Virginia Resolutions.

3. Freedom of speech and the press are essential rights because governments must be closely watched. The Alien and Sedition Acts violated this principle.

4. The scope and activities of the federal government should be reduced and be only what is specifically permitted in the Constitution. The president should practice republican simplicity.

C. THE LOUISIANA PURCHASE, 1803

1. The Louisiana Purchase had its origins in Jefferson's desire to acquire the Port of New Orleans to provide an outlet for Western crops.

2. The failure of the French army to suppress a slave revolt in Haiti motivated Napoleon to sell the vast Louisiana Territory.

3. Purchasing the Louisiana Territory violated Jefferson's belief in a strict interpretation of the Constitution. As a result, Jefferson had to be pragmatic and do what was in the best interest of the country.

4. Jefferson hoped to perpetuate an agricultural society and strengthen the Democratic-Republican Party by making abundant lands available to future generations.

5. The Louisiana Purchase was America's largest acquisition of territory. The price was roughly three cents an acre.

6. Jefferson commissioned the Corps of Discovery, led by Lewis and Clark, to explore and map the region, which bordered on British and Spanish western territories.

II. THE MARSHALL COURT

A. BELIEF IN A STRONG CENTRAL GOVERNMENT

1. Chief Justice John Marshall, an ardent Federalist, believed that a strong central government best served the nation's interests.

2. Marshall opposed states' rights and consistently ruled in ways to strengthen the federal government.

B. *MARBURY v. MADISON*, 1803

1. Adams appointed Federalist judges as he left office. Jefferson refused to allow them to take office.

2. By overruling the Judiciary Act of 1789, this case established the principle of judicial review, the right of the Supreme Court to rule that a law is unconstitutional.

C. OPPOSITION TO STATES' RIGHTS

1. Under Marshall's leadership, the Supreme Court upheld the supremacy of federal legislation over state legislation.

2. For example, in *Dartmouth College v. Woodward*, the Marshall Court ruled that a state could not encroach on a previously existing contract.

D. ECONOMIC NATIONALISM

1. Marshall was an economic nationalist who promoted the growth of business enterprises.

2. For example, in *McCulloch v. Maryland*, the Court struck down a Maryland law taxing the Baltimore branch of the National Bank.

CONTENT REVIEW

John Marshall has cast a long shadow across both American judicial history and the APUSH exam. Many previous exams have included a question about **Marbury v. Madison** *and the concept of judicial review. It is also important to remember that Marshall was a proponent of a strong central government and an opponent of states' rights.*

III. THE WAR OF 1812

A. CAUSES OF THE WAR

1. British impressments of American seamen

2. Desire for Canadian land

3. British interference with American commerce

4. British aid to Native Americans in the Ohio River Valley

B. CONSEQUENCES OF THE WAR

1. Contributed to the demise of the Federalist Party

2. Intensified nationalist feelings

3. Promoted industrialization

4. Advanced the career of victorious General Andrew Jackson

 IV. THE PRESIDENCY OF JAMES MONROE, 1817–1825

A. CLAY'S AMERICAN SYSTEM

1. Henry Clay's plan to aid American businesses included three basic components:

   ▸ The need for an improved transportation system; Henry Clay believed that new transportation links would promote trade and unite the various sections of the country.

   ▸ High tariffs on imported goods to protect U.S. manufacturers from foreign competition.

   ▸ A national bank (the Second National Bank was chartered in 1816; the First National Bank expired in 1811).

2. Because of its dependence on agricultural plantations and slave labor, the South benefited least from the era of internal improvements.

3. The Northeast and the West became more closely aligned as the American System developed, especially after the completion of the Erie Canal in 1825.

4. Clay's Second National Bank proved to be very controversial before it was vetoed by Andrew Jackson in 1832. Its loose lending standards contributed to the Panic of 1819.

B. AN ERA OF GOOD FEELINGS OR RISING TENSIONS?

1. The demise of the Federalist Party left the Democratic-Republicans in control of Congress and the presidency.

2. The illusion of a national political consensus was shattered by contentious issues such as protective tariffs, federal aid for internal improvements, and the expansion of slavery into the new territories.

C. THE MISSOURI COMPROMISE OF 1820

1. The Missouri Compromise settled the first major nineteenth-century conflict over slavery.

2. Maine entered the Union as a free state.

3. Missouri entered the Union as a slave state, thus maintaining the balance between free and slave states in the Senate.

4. The compromise closed the remaining territory of the Louisiana Purchase above the 36°30′ line to slavery.

Feelings were not always so harmonious during the so-called Era of Good Feelings. Clay's American System and the Missouri Compromise of 1820 both generated heated debate . . . and a large number of APUSH questions. Make sure you review the purposes of Clay's American System and the provisions of the Missouri Compromise.

D. THE MONROE DOCTRINE, 1823

1. The Monroe Doctrine was a declaration of American principles that asserted U.S. independence from Europe in foreign policy.

2. It asserted that the political system in the Western Hemisphere is different and separate from that of Europe, reinforcing the same theme in Washington's Farewell Address.

3. It warned European nations against further colonial ventures into the Western Hemisphere.

4. It promised that the United States would not interfere in the internal affairs of European nations.

 ## V. KEY TENETS OF JACKSONIAN DEMOCRACY

A. BELIEF IN THE COMMON MAN

1. Jackson's followers had great respect for the values and abilities of the common man.

2. Andrew Jackson was seen as an advocate for the interests of ordinary citizens and an opponent of the Eastern moneyed interests.

B. EXPANDED SUFFRAGE

1. Jackson and the Democrats dramatically expanded white male suffrage.

2. During the Federalist Era, caucuses of party leaders selected candidates. During the Jackson administration, nominating conventions replaced legislative caucuses.

C. PATRONAGE

1. Jackson supported the spoils system—the policy of placing political supporters in office.

2. Jackson believed that political supporters should be rewarded with government jobs.

D. OPPOSITION TO PRIVILEGED ELITES

1. As a champion of the common man, Jackson despised the special privileges of the Eastern elite.

2. Whenever there was a conflict between moneyed interests and the common folk, Jackson sought ways to help the common folk.

VI. THE TARIFF OF ABOMINATIONS AND THE NULLIFICATION CRISIS

A. THE TARIFF OF ABOMINATIONS, 1828

1. The tariffs passed between 1816 and 1828 were the first tariffs in American history whose primary purpose was the protection of home industry rather than raising revenue.

2. The Northeast benefited from tariffs; they were unpopular in the South, which had few manufacturers.

3. The Tariff of Abominations forced John C. Calhoun of South Carolina to formulate his doctrine of nullification.

B. THE DOCTRINE OF NULLIFICATION

1. Developed by John C. Calhoun, the doctrine of nullification drew heavily on the states' rights arguments advanced by Jefferson and Madison in the Kentucky and Virginia Resolutions.

2. In the *South Carolina Exposition and Protest*, Calhoun argued that a state could refuse to obey an act of Congress that it considers unconstitutional.

C. OPPOSITION TO NULLIFICATION

1. In the Webster-Hayne Debate, Daniel Webster forcefully rejected nullification. Webster concluded with his great exhortation, "Liberty and Union, now and forever, one and inseparable." Webster's region, the North, generally benefited from both high tariffs and the national bank; Hayne's region, the South, did not.

2. Jackson opposed South Carolina's efforts and threatened military action if the tariffs were not collected.

VII. THE BANK WAR

A. JACKSON'S VETO

1. Jackson vigorously opposed the bill to re-charter the Second Bank of the United States (BUS).

2. Jackson believed that the bank represented individuals who had special privileges. He argued that the BUS was beneficial to advocates of "hard money" and thus harmful to the interests of the common people who elected him.

B. CONSEQUENCES

1. Jackson supported the removal of federal deposits from the Bank of the United States.

2. Jackson's attack on the BUS caused an expansion of credit and speculation by (mostly) unregulated state banks.

3. The number of state banks (often known as pet banks), each issuing its own paper currency, increased.

4. Jackson's war on the BUS was an important catalyst for the emergence of a competitive two-party system. The Whigs hated Jackson and supported Henry Clay and his American System.

5. Jackson's policies (which allowed the state banks to lend money too aggressively) helped lead to the Panic of 1837 and the collapse of many state banks.

 VIII. JACKSON AND THE FORCED REMOVAL OF NATIVE AMERICANS

A. *WORCESTER v. GEORGIA*, 1831

1. The Cherokee differed from other Native American tribes in that they mounted a court challenge to a removal order.

2. In the case of *Worcester v. Georgia*, the United States Supreme Court upheld the rights of the Cherokee to their tribal lands.

B. JACKSON AND THE CHEROKEE

1. Jackson's antipathy toward Native Americans was well known. In one speech he declared, "I have long viewed treaties with American Indians as an absurdity not to be reconciled to the principles of our government."

2. Jackson refused to recognize the Court's decision, allegedly declaring, "John Marshall has made his decision: now let him enforce it."

Normally, very few APUSH questions are devoted to specific presidents. Andrew Jackson and Abraham Lincoln are the exceptions. Because of his pivotal role in the nullification crisis, the bank war, and the forced removal of Native Americans, a number of APUSH questions focus on Andrew Jackson and his policies.

C. THE TRAIL OF TEARS

1. Jackson's Native American policy resulted in the removal of the Cherokee from their homeland to settlements across the Mississippi River.

2. The Trail of Tears refers to the route taken by a number of tribes as they were relocated to the Indian Territory of Oklahoma.

3. Approximately one-quarter of the participants died on the Trail of Tears.

IX. THE TRANSPORTATION REVOLUTION

A. NEW DEVELOPMENTS

1. Completed in 1825, the Erie Canal sparked a period of canal building that lasted until 1850.

2. Steamboats came into wide use in the 1820s and 1830s.

3. The first railroad appeared in the United States in 1828. Within thirty years, the United States had built 30,000 miles of track.

B. CONSEQUENCES

1. The Erie Canal strengthened commercial and political ties between New York City and the growing cities on the Great Lakes, and it connected the Eastern seaboard with New Orleans.

2. Canals helped open the West to settlement and trade.

3. Steamboats dramatically increased river traffic while significantly lowering the cost of river transportation.

4. Like the canals, the railroads gave farmers in the Midwest easier access to urban markets in the East.

5. Canals, steamboats, and railroads had the least impact on the South; the East and West continued to link over common economic and political interests, while the South grew increasingly independent.

X. TEXAS INDEPENDENCE FIGHT, 1836

A. AMERICAN SETTLERS IN MEXICAN TEXAS

1. Led by Stephen Austin, thousands of Americans migrated to Texas, which, at the time, was part of Mexico.

2. Mexican laws outlawing slavery and requiring settlers to convert to Catholicism antagonized settlers.

B. BATTLES AND THE ESTABLISHMENT OF THE LONE STAR REPUBLIC

1. After a group of American settlers declared their independence, Mexican forces overwhelmed a garrison at the Alamo in San Antonio.

2. The Mexican commander Santa Anna eventually surrendered and the Lone Star Republic was established, though it did not enter the Union as Texas until 1845.

XI. TRANSCENDENTALISM AND UTOPIAN COMMUNITIES

A. TRANSCENDENTALISM

1. Transcendentalism was a philosophical and literary movement of the 1800s that emphasized living a simple life while celebrating the truth found in nature and in personal emotion and imagination.

2. Henry David Thoreau and Ralph Waldo Emerson were the leading transcendentalist writers.

B. UTOPIAN COMMUNITIES

1. Utopians shared a faith in perfectionism—that is, the belief that humans have the capacity to achieve a better life through conscious acts of will.

2. The best-known utopian communities included Brook Farm, New Harmony, and the Oneida Community.

3. Utopian communities strove to escape the competitiveness of American life, regulate moral behavior, and create cooperative lifestyles.

XII. RELIGIOUS AND SOCIAL REFORM

A. THE SECOND GREAT AWAKENING

1. A series of frontier revivals and religious enthusiasm, with an emphasis on personal conversion, swept through the United States.

CONTENT REVIEW

2. The Second Great Awakening played an important role in making Americans aware of the moral issues posed by slavery and spurred other social reforms.

3. Even though they could not vote, women and blacks played a prominent role in the revivals, building on the new spirit of participatory democracy in the United States.

B. REFORM MOVEMENTS

1. Dorothea Dix attempted to raise awareness about the mistreatment of those in mental institutions.

2. Horace Mann pushed for universal public education with a secular and practical focus.

3. Temperance societies attempted to regulate the sale of alcohol.

4. Prison reform advocates urged that jail time be used to rehabilitate and reform inmates.

XIII. THE ROLE OF WOMEN IN ANTEBELLUM AMERICA

A. THE CULT OF DOMESTICITY/REPUBLICAN MOTHERHOOD

1. American women could not vote, serve on juries, or perform other civic tasks. These restrictions raised the question of what role women should play in the new republic.

2. The concept of republican motherhood advanced the idea that women did have a vital role to play as wives and mothers. Proponents argued that women should be educated to rear their children to be virtuous citizens of the new American republic. The republican mother should be concerned with domestic, family, and religious affairs.

Some students are surprised when they encounter APUSH questions on the cult of domesticity/republican motherhood. APUSH exams often have one, possibly even two multiple-choice questions on this concept. Test writers have used straightforward definitions, quotes, and even pictures to see if students can identify the cult of domesticity/republican motherhood.

B. FACTORY WORKERS IN LOWELL

1. During the first half of the nineteenth century, textile mills in Lowell, Massachusetts, relied heavily on a labor force of young, unmarried women.

2. Prior to the Civil War, Irish immigrants began to replace New England farm girls in the textile mills.

3. Industrial expansion pushed Lowell's population from about 2,500 in 1826 to over 33,000 in 1850, when Lowell was Massachusetts' second-largest city.

XIV. THE CHANGING ROLE OF WOMEN IN ANTEBELLUM AMERICA

A. CHARACTERISTICS OF THE WOMEN'S MOVEMENT

1. The movement was led by middle-class women and promoted a broad-based platform of legal and educational rights.

2. It had close links with the antislavery and temperance movements and was part of the reform movements of the Jacksonian Era.

B. THE SENECA FALLS CONVENTION, 1848

1. Organized and led by Elizabeth Cady Stanton and Lucretia Mott, this convention called for women's rights in the following areas:

   ▶ Women's suffrage

CONTENT REVIEW

‣ Women's right to retain property after marriage

‣ Greater divorce and child custody rights

‣ Equal educational opportunities

2. The "Declaration of Sentiments and Resolutions" issued by the Seneca Falls Convention demanded greater rights for women. The declaration's first sentence clearly stated this goal: "We hold these truths to be self-evident: that all men and women are created equal."

It is important to know what reforms were advocated by the Seneca Falls Convention. It is also important to know what reforms the convention did not advocate. For example, the Seneca Falls Convention did not call for more liberal abortion laws or equal pay for equal work, but it did focus on education, basic legal rights, and suffrage.

PERIOD 5
1844–1877

Key Concepts†

Concept 1: The United States became more connected with the world as it pursued an expansionist foreign policy in the Western Hemisphere and emerged as the destination for many immigrants from other countries.

Concept 2: Intensified by expansion and deepening regional divisions, debates over slavery and other economic, cultural, and political issues led the nation into civil war.

Concept 3: The Union victory in the Civil War and the contested Reconstruction of the South settled the issues of slavery and secession, but they did not resolve many questions about the power of the federal government and citizenship rights.

I. MANIFEST DESTINY AND TERRITORIAL EXPANSION

A. THE RIGHT TO EXPAND

1. Coined by newspaper editor John O'Sullivan in 1845, the term *Manifest Destiny* suggested that God had ordained the United States to expand westward to the Pacific Ocean and settle all lands not already under its control.

2. Manifest Destiny was used to gain public support for American territorial expansion in Texas, Oregon, and the territory controlled by Mexico in the Southwest.

---

† © 2014 The College Board.

B. TEXAS

1. President Jackson opposed the admission of Texas into the Union even though he favored territorial expansion. Jackson feared that debate over the admission of Texas would ignite controversy over slavery.

2. Texas existed as the Lone Star Republic until 1845 because Americans were divided over the issue of admitting another slave state into the Union.

C. OREGON TERRITORY

1. During the 1844 election campaign, the slogan "fifty-four forty or fight" referred to Democrat James Polk's promise to take all of the Oregon land under dispute between the United States and Britain.

2. The United States and Britain reached a compromise that established the northern boundary of Oregon at the 49th parallel.

D. THE MEXICAN WAR, 1846–1848

1. President Polk justified the Mexican-American War by claiming that Mexican troops had illegally crossed into American territory, where they attacked and killed American soldiers. Hostilities had thus been forced on the United States by the shedding of "American blood upon the American soil."

2. Whigs opposed the Mexican-American War because they saw it as an attempt to grab more land for slaveholders. Congressman Abraham Lincoln and author Henry David Thoreau both spoke out against the war.

3. Signed in 1848, the Treaty of Guadalupe Hidalgo ended the Mexican-American War. Under the terms of the treaty, the United States gained California and New Mexico (including present-day Nevada, Utah, and Arizona, as well as parts of Colorado and Wyoming) and recognition of the Rio Grande as the southern boundary of Texas.

4. The Wilmot Proviso called for the prohibition of slavery in lands acquired from Mexico in the Mexican War. Although it never became federal law, it was eventually endorsed by the legislatures of all but one of the free states, and it came to symbolize the polarizing issue of extending slavery into the territories.

The Wilmot Proviso is so well known that it is easy to believe that it became a law. In fact, it did not. Although the House passed the Wilmot Proviso twice, the Senate rejected it. APUSH test writers use the phrase "passage of the Wilmot Proviso" as a tempting—but incorrect—answer. Note that the Wilmot Proviso did not support popular sovereignty.

II. ABOLITION AND ABOLITIONISTS

A. AMERICAN COLONIZATION SOCIETY

1. Founded in 1817, the American Colonization Society worked to return freed slaves to the west coast of Africa.

2. It was primarily led by middle-class evangelicals and had many prominent supporters, including President James Monroe and Henry Clay.

3. At least 13,000 slaves were repatriated to Liberia in West Africa.

B. WILLIAM LLOYD GARRISON

1. Garrison was the editor of the radical abolitionist newspaper named *The Liberator* and a founder of the American Anti-Slavery Society.

2. Published in January 1831, Garrison used the first issue to call for the "immediate and uncompensated emancipation of the slaves."

3. In that same issue, Garrison further wrote: "Let Southern oppressors tremble . . . I will be as harsh as Truth and as uncompromising as Justice . . . I am in earnest—I will not retreat a single inch—and I WILL BE HEARD!"

4. Garrison's support of women's rights and radical abolitionism caused the American Anti-Slavery Society to split into rival factions.

C. FREDERICK DOUGLASS

1. Frederick Douglass was the most prominent black abolitionist during the antebellum period. He had his own publication, which he called the *North Star*.

2. Although best known as an abolitionist, Douglass championed equal rights for women and Native Americans. He often declared, "I would unite with anybody to do right and with nobody to do wrong."

D. SARAH MOORE GRIMKÉ

1. Grimké was one of the first women to support both abolition and women's rights publicly.

2. "I ask no favor for my sex," declared Grimké. "I surrender not our claim to equality. All I ask of our brethren is that they will take their feet off our necks."

3. She and her sister Angelina, another well-known abolitionist, were the daughters of a prominent South Carolina slaveholder.

Test Tip

Most APUSH students study Frederick Douglass, and a significant number have read portions of his autobiography. In contrast, many students have less familiarity with William Lloyd Garrison. Be sure to focus on Garrison as you prepare for the exam. Although Frederick Douglass has a prominent position in most textbooks and courses, APUSH test writers have written a number of questions about Garrison.

III. THE COMPROMISE OF 1850

A. NEGOTIATIONS

1. Stephen A. Douglas, Daniel Webster, Henry Clay, and John C. Calhoun all played key roles in the negotiations that resulted in the passage of the Compromise of 1850.

2. While the Compromise did not solve any of the problems presented by the slave question, it postponed war for a decade between the North and the South.

B. PROVISIONS

1. Admission of California as a free state

2. Abolition of the slave trade in the District of Columbia

3. Passage of a more stringent Fugitive Slave Act

4. Establishment of territorial governments in New Mexico and Utah, without an immediate decision on the status of slavery

IV. POPULAR SOVEREIGNTY AND THE KANSAS-NEBRASKA ACT, 1854

A. POPULAR SOVEREIGNTY

1. Senator Stephen A. Douglas was the leading proponent of popular sovereignty, which attempted to settle the question of whether it was legal to establish slavery in the Western territories.

2. The principle stated that the settlers of a given territory would have the sole right to decide whether slavery would be permitted there.

B. THE KANSAS-NEBRASKA ACT, 1854

1. The act proposed that the Territory of Nebraska would be divided into two territories—Kansas and Nebraska.

2. Their status as slave or free states would be determined by the residents of the new states as they entered the Union.

C. CONSEQUENCES OF THE KANSAS-NEBRASKA ACT

1. The act did the following:

   ▸ Repealed the Missouri Compromise of 1820, thus heightening sectional tensions

   ▸ Permitted the expansion of slavery beyond the Southern states

   ▸ Led to a divisive debate over the expansion of slavery into the territories

   ▸ Ignited a bloody contest for control over Kansas (known as Bleeding Kansas)

   ▸ Split the Democratic Party

   ▸ Brought about the end of the Whig Party and sparked the formation of the Republican Party

V. THE *DRED SCOTT* CASE, 1857

A. THE RULING

1. Dred Scott was a slave and thus could not sue in federal court.

2. Under the Constitution, slaves were private property and thus could be taken into any territory and legally held there in slavery.

3. Slaves could not be taken from their masters, regardless of a territory's free or slave status. As such, it could be concluded that "once a slave, always a slave."

B. THE CONSEQUENCES

1. The ruling invalidated the Northwest Ordinance of 1787 and the Missouri Compromise of 1820 by which Congress had regulated slavery's presence by the territories.

2. The ruling became a major issue in the Lincoln–Douglas debates.

3. The decision widened the gap between North and South, thus bringing them closer to war.

> *It is a good idea to keep straight the compromises, acts, and Supreme Court decisions that affected slavery. The Missouri Compromise of 1820, the Kansas-Nebraska Act, and the Dred Scott decision all permitted the expansion of slavery beyond the Southern states. The Compromise of 1850 brought California into the Union as a free state, but it did not restrict slavery in other territories.*

VI. JOHN BROWN'S RAID

A. RADICAL ABOLITIONIST JOHN BROWN PLANNED AN UPRISING

1. Brown and his followers seized a federal arsenal in Harpers Ferry, Virginia.

2. Brown hoped to spur a slave revolt throughout the South.

3. The raid failed to liberate any slaves, and Brown and his supporters were captured.

B. CONSEQUENCES

1. Brown was executed after making an eloquent plea for the abolition of slavery.

2. He became a martyr to abolitionists in the North.

3. He became a symbol to the South of the willingness of extreme abolitionists to use violence to end slavery.

CONTENT REVIEW

VII. THE ELECTION OF 1860

A. REPUBLICANS AND DEMOCRATS

1. Led by Abraham Lincoln, the Republicans accepted slavery where it existed but opposed the expansion of slavery into the territories.

2. The Democratic Party split. Northern Democrats supported Stephen A. Douglas and popular sovereignty. Southern Democrats supported John C. Breckinridge, the extension of slavery into the territories, and the annexation of Cuba.

B. CONSEQUENCES

1. Lincoln won the electoral vote but received less than 40 percent of the popular vote.

2. Led by South Carolina, seven Southern states seceded from the Union.

 VIII. THE CIVIL WAR

A. ADVANTAGES OF THE NORTH

1. An extensive railroad network

2. A strong industrial base

3. A superior navy

4. A larger population

5. An abundant supply of food

6. An established, functioning central government

B. DISADVANTAGES OF THE NORTH

1. A shortage of experienced and skilled military commanders

2. A divided population that did not fully support the war; as such, it lacked a unified war aim

C. ADVANTAGES OF THE SOUTH

1. A defensive war fought on its home territory

2. A long coastline that would be difficult to blockade

3. An important cash crop in cotton

4. Experienced and skilled military commanders

5. A close economic relationship with Great Britain

6. A unified war aim based on defending the strong belief in Southern economic and cultural values, including the necessity of slavery

D. DISADVANTAGES OF THE SOUTH

1. A smaller population than the North

2. A smaller industrial base than the North

3. Lack of a diversified economy

IX. THE BORDER STATES

A. IMPORTANCE

1. Strategic location

2. Important industrial and agricultural resources

3. Alienating their residents might cause them to join the Confederacy

B. KEY BORDER STATES

1. Kentucky

2. Maryland

3. Missouri

4. Delaware

X. THE BATTLE OF ANTIETAM AND THE EMANCIPATION PROCLAMATION

A. THE BATTLE OF ANTIETAM

1. The Union victory persuaded England and France to remain neutral. While both European powers saw advantages in a divided America, they followed a cautious policy toward both the North and the South.

2. The Union victory enabled Lincoln to issue the Emancipation Proclamation.

> *The Battle of Gettysburg and Vicksburg and Sherman's March to the Sea are all pivotal events that played a key role in the Civil War. Like other military battles, however, they are often totally ignored by APUSH test writers. Antietam is the only Civil War battle that has appeared on released AP exams. Keep in mind that the Union victory convinced England and France to remain neutral, and enabled Lincoln to issue the Emancipation Proclamation.*

B. THE EMANCIPATION PROCLAMATION

1. Lincoln delayed issuing the Emancipation Proclamation because he didn't want to antagonize slave owners in the border states.

2. The North originally went to war to preserve the Union. The Emancipation Proclamation strengthened the Union's moral cause and changed the purpose of the war from merely preserving the Union to include ending slavery.

3. The Emancipation Proclamation rallied antislavery support in England and France and persuaded those nations to withhold support for the Confederacy.

4. The Emancipation Proclamation did not free any slaves in the border states.

5. The Emancipation Proclamation actually freed only the slaves in areas of Confederate states that were under Union control.

*It is important to focus on what the Emancipation Procla-
mation did and did not do. It did significantly enhance the
Union's moral cause; however, it did not actually free many
slaves because the South ignored it. It was much stronger
on proclamation than on emancipation. Slavery was legally
abolished by the Thirteenth Amendment in 1865.*

XI. KEY POLITICAL ACTIONS DURING THE CIVIL WAR

A. CONGRESSIONAL ACTIONS

1. Congress established a national banking system to provide a uniform national currency.

2. Congress chartered two corporations—the Union Pacific Railroad and the Central Pacific Railroad—to build a transcontinental railroad connecting Omaha, Nebraska, with Sacramento, California.

3. Congress passed the Homestead Act of 1862, offering cheap—sometimes free—land to people who would settle the West and improve their property.

4. Congress passed high tariffs to protect U.S. industry from foreign competition.

5. Given the foregoing, it should be noted that Abraham Lincoln carried on Federalist Party economic principles that were first developed by Alexander Hamilton and then kept alive, for example, by John Marshall, Henry Clay (with his American System), and Daniel Webster.

B. EXPANSION OF PRESIDENTIAL POWER

1. Lincoln found that the Civil War required active and prompt presidential action.

2. Lincoln suspended the writ of habeas corpus for everyone living between Washington, D.C., and Philadelphia.

3. He issued the Emancipation Proclamation as a war necessity because its constitutionality was questioned.

XII. RECONSTRUCTION ERA AMENDMENTS

A. THE THIRTEENTH AMENDMENT, 1865

1. Abolished slavery and involuntary servitude

2. Completed the work of the Emancipation Proclamation

B. THE FOURTEENTH AMENDMENT, 1868

1. Declared the former slaves to be citizens, thus invalidating the Dred Scott decision

2. Provided for "equal protection of the laws" for all citizens

3. Enforced congressional legislation guaranteeing civil rights to former slaves

C. THE FIFTEENTH AMENDMENT, 1870

1. The amendment provided suffrage for black males.

2. Some women's rights supporters, including Lucy Stone, Julia Ward Howe, and Frederick Douglass, supported the amendment.

3. Other women's rights supporters, led by Susan B. Anthony and Elizabeth Cady Stanton, opposed the amendment. They argued, without success, that a universal suffrage amendment, which included women, was needed.

 XIII. RADICAL RECONSTRUCTION

A. CAUSES

1. Some former Confederates were elected to Congress.

2. Black Codes limiting the rights of former slaves were enacted in Southern states.

3. Race riots broke out in New Orleans and Memphis.

4. There were attempts in the South to undermine the Fourteenth Amendment.

B. PROGRAMS AND POLICIES

1. Congress ordered military occupation of the South, dividing it into five military districts.

2. Punishment of Confederate leaders became policy.

3. Restrictions were placed on the power of President Andrew Johnson.

4. The House of Representatives impeached Johnson because he obstructed enforcement of the Reconstruction Acts.

C. ACHIEVEMENTS

1. Assisted by the Freedmen's Bureau, public school systems in the Southern states were improved.

2. African Americans were elected to the House and Senate.

XIV. IMPEACHMENT OF ANDREW JOHNSON

A. RADICALS OPPOSED JOHNSON

1. Andrew Johnson of Tennessee became president upon Lincoln's assassination.

2. Radical Republicans distrusted him and felt he did not sufficiently support Reconstruction programs.

B. IMPEACHMENT TRIAL

1. Republicans passed the Tenure of Office Act, knowing Johnson would violate it.

2. In the nation's first presidential impeachment trial, Johnson was cleared by just one vote.

XV. THE PLIGHT OF AFRICAN AMERICANS

A. FROM SLAVES TO SHARECROPPERS

1. The majority of freedmen entered sharecropping arrangements with their former masters.

CONTENT REVIEW

2. Sharecropping led to a cycle of debt and depression for Southern tenant farmers.

3. Contrary to a widespread rumor, the freedmen did not receive "40 acres and a mule." In hindsight, it appears that this type of wealth redistribution would have been required for the freed slaves to have achieved economic independence.

4. The Panic of 1873 and the subsequent depression it caused are generally considered key factors in explaining why so many Northerners abandoned their efforts to help the freedmen.

B. BLACK CODES

1. The codes were passed by Southern state legislatures and intended to limit the socioeconomic opportunities and freedoms open to blacks.

2. The codes forced blacks to work under conditions that closely resembled slavery.

 XVI. THE END OF RECONSTRUCTION

A. THE ELECTION OF 1876

1. Democratic candidate Samuel Tilden polled more popular votes than Rutherford B. Hayes.

2. Tilden won 184 of the 185 electoral votes needed for election.

3. There were twenty disputed votes in four states, three of which were in the South.

B. THE COMPROMISE OF 1877

1. Democrats agreed that Hayes would take office.

PERIOD 6
1865–1898

Key Concepts[†]

Concept 1: The rise of big business in the United States encouraged massive migrations and urbanization, sparked government and popular efforts to reshape the U.S. economy and environment, and renewed debates over U.S. national identity.

Concept 2: The emergence of an industrial culture in the United States led to both greater opportunities for, and restrictions on, immigrants, minorities, and women.

Concept 3: The Gilded Age witnessed new cultural and intellectual movements in tandem with political debates over economic and social policies.

I. BIG BUSINESS

A. THE CONSOLIDATION OF BIG BUSINESS

1. *Vertical integration* occurs when a company controls the sources, production, and distribution of its product. For example, Andrew Carnegie used vertical integration to gain control over the U.S. steel industry.

2. *Horizontal integration* occurs when one company gains control over other companies that produce the same product. For example, John D. Rockefeller used horizontal integration to gain control over oil production in the United States.

[†] © 2014 The College Board.

3. By the end of the nineteenth century, monopolies and trusts exercised a significant degree of control over key aspects of the U.S. economy.

B. CONSEQUENCES OF CONSOLIDATION

1. Corporations built large, systematically organized factories where work was increasingly performed by machines and unskilled workers.

2. Corporations introduced systems of scientific management, also known as Taylorism, to increase factory production and lower labor costs.

3. Corporations accumulated vast sums of investment capital.

4. Corporations used the railroads to help develop national markets for their goods.

C. CELEBRATING AMERICA'S INDUSTRIAL SUCCESS

1. The World's Columbian Exposition of 1893 in Chicago showcased America's industrial development.

2. The popular Horatio Alger, Jr. stories provided concrete examples of the ideal of the self-made man; Andrew Carnegie was the most prominent example.

II. LABOR AND LABOR UNIONS, 1865–1900

A. KEY TRENDS

1. Immigrants, women, and children significantly expanded the labor force.

2. Machines increasingly replaced skilled artisans.

3. Large bureaucratic corporations dominated the U.S. economy.

4. Corporations developed national and even international markets for their goods.

B. THE KNIGHTS OF LABOR

1. Membership in the Knights of Labor, led by Terence V. Powderly, increased significantly and quickly, peaking at 730,000 members in 1886.

2. The Knights grew rapidly because of their open-membership policy, the continuing industrialization of the U.S. economy, and the growth of the urban population.

3. Unskilled and semiskilled workers, including women, immigrants, and African Americans, were welcomed into the organization.

4. The Knights were idealists who believed they could eliminate conflict between labor and management. Their goal was to create a cooperative society in which laborers, not capitalists, owned the industries in which they worked.

5. The Haymarket Square riot in 1886 was unfairly blamed on the Knights. As a result, the public associated them with anarchists, and membership rapidly declined.

C. THE INDUSTRIAL WORKERS OF THE WORLD

1. The Industrial Workers of the World (IWW) was led by "Mother" Jones, Elizabeth Flynn, and Big Bill Haywood.

2. Like the Knights of Labor, the IWW strove to unite all laborers, including unskilled African Americans, who were excluded from craft unions.

3. The IWW's motto was "An injury to one is an injury to all," and its goal was to create "One Big Union."

4. Unlike the Knights, the IWW (or Wobblies) embraced the rhetoric of class conflict and endorsed violent tactics.

5. IWW membership probably never exceeded 150,000 workers. The organization collapsed during World War I.

D. THE AMERICAN FEDERATION OF LABOR

1. The American Federation of Labor (AFL) was led by Samuel Gompers, the leader of the Cigar Makers Union.

2. The AFL was an alliance of skilled workers in craft unions; it did *not* include unskilled workers.

3. Under Gompers' leadership, the AFL concentrated on bread-and-butter issues such as higher wages, shorter hours, and better working conditions.

It is very important to understand the similarities and differences among the Knights of Labor, the Industrial Workers of the World, and the American Federation of Labor. All three were dedicated to organizing laborers. The Knights and the IWW both attempted to organize all skilled and unskilled workers into one union. However, the Knights strove for a cooperative society, while the IWW embraced class conflict and violent tactics. In contrast, the AFL organized skilled workers, repudiated violence, and fought for higher wages and better working conditions.

E. THE PULLMAN STRIKE, 1894

1. During the late nineteenth century, the U.S. labor movement experienced a number of violent strikes. The two best-known strikes were the Homestead Strike (1892) and the Pullman Strike (1894).

2. When the national economy fell into a depression, the Pullman Palace Car Company cut wages while maintaining rents and prices in a company town where 12,000 workers lived. This action precipitated the Pullman Strike.

3. The Pullman Strike halted a substantial portion of U.S. railroad commerce.

4. The strike ended when President Cleveland ordered federal troops to Chicago, ostensibly to protect rail-carried mail but, in reality, to crush the strike.

5. In a famous case heard by the Supreme Court in 1895 (*In re Debs*), the Supreme Court allowed the use of court injunctions to end strikes; this decision was a major blow to unions.

III. IMMIGRATION

A. THE NEW IMMIGRANTS

1. Prior to 1880, most immigrants to the United States came from the British Isles and Western Europe.

2. Beginning in the 1880s, a new wave of immigrants left Europe for the United States. The so-called New Immigrants came from small towns and villages in Southern and Eastern Europe. The majority lived in Italy, Russia, Poland, and Austria-Hungary.

3. The New Immigrants settled primarily in large cities in the Northeast and Midwest, where they often took low-paying factory jobs and lived in slums.

4. Very few New Immigrants settled in the South.

B. THE CHINESE EXCLUSION ACT OF 1882

1. This was the first law in U.S. history to exclude a group from the United States because of ethnic background.

2. The act prohibited the immigration of Chinese to the United States.

3. Working-class Americans who felt threatened by Chinese workers strongly supported the law.

4. Support for the law was particularly strong in California.

C. NATIVIST OPPOSITION TO THE NEW IMMIGRANTS

1. Nativists had previously opposed Irish and German Catholic immigrants.

2. Nativists opposed the New Immigrants for the following reasons:

   ▸ The immigrants were mostly Catholic and Jewish.

   ▸ They spoke different languages and practiced different cultural traditions.

   ▸ They did not understand American political traditions.

> ▸ They threatened to take away jobs because they were willing to work for low wages.

IV. THE NEW INDUSTRIAL ORDER: SUPPORTERS AND REFORMERS

A. SOCIAL DARWINISM

1. Social Darwinism is the belief that individuals, groups, and peoples are subject to the same Darwinian laws of natural selection as plants and animals.

2. Wealthy business and industrial leaders used Social Darwinism to justify their success.

3. Social Darwinists believed that industrial and urban problems are part of a natural evolutionary process that humans cannot control.

B. GOSPEL OF WEALTH

1. This gospel was promoted by Andrew Carnegie.

2. It expressed the belief that, as the guardians of society's wealth, the rich have a duty to serve society.

3. Over his lifetime, Carnegie donated more than $350 million to support libraries, schools, peace initiatives, and the arts.

V. AGRARIAN DISCONTENT

A. CAUSES OF AGRARIAN DISCONTENT

1. Discontent was based on the beliefs that

   > ▸ Railroads were using discriminatory rates to exploit small farmers.

   > ▸ Big business used high tariffs to exploit small farmers.

   > ▸ A deflationary monetary policy based on gold hurt farmers (who wanted an inflationary monetary policy

based on silver, which would have allowed them to repay their debts in lesser-valued dollars).

▸ Corporations charged exorbitant prices for fertilizer and farm machinery.

B. THE POPULIST OR PEOPLE'S PARTY

1. The Populist Party attempted to unite discontented farmers.

2. It attempted to improve their economic conditions and supported the following:

   ▸ Increasing the money supply with the free and unlimited coinage of silver and gold at the legal ratio of 16:1

   ▸ Using the Interstate Commerce Act of 1887 to regulate railroads and prevent discrimination against small customers

   ▸ Organizing cooperative marketing societies

   ▸ Supporting the candidacy of William Jennings Bryan in the 1896 presidential election

C. REASONS THE POPULIST PARTY FAILED

1. Western and Southern farmers did not agree on political strategies.

2. Racism prevented poor white and black farmers from working together.

3. The dramatic increases in urban population caused by the wave of New Immigrants led to higher prices for agricultural products.

4. The discovery of gold in the Yukon increased the supply of gold, thus easing farmers' access to credit.

5. The Democratic Party absorbed many Populist programs.

6. William Jennings Bryan lost the 1896 presidential election to William McKinley and the Republicans.

PERIOD 7
1890–1945

Key Concepts†

Concept 1: Governmental, political, and social organizations struggled to address the effects of large-scale industrialization, economic uncertainty, and related social changes such as urbanization and mass migration.

Concept 2: A revolution in communications and transportation technology helped to create a new mass culture and spread modern values and ideas, even as cultural conflicts between and among groups increased under the pressure of migration, world wars, and economic distress.

Concept 3: Global conflicts over resources, territories, and ideologies renewed debates over the nation's values and its role in the world while simultaneously propelling the United States into a dominant international military, political, cultural, and economic position.

I. LATE NINETEENTH-CENTURY URBAN REFORMERS

A. SOCIAL GOSPEL

1. The Social Gospel was a reform movement based on the belief that Christians have a responsibility to confront social problems.

2. Christian ministers, including Baptist minister Walter Rauschenbusch, were among the leaders of this movement.

3. Soup kitchens and storefront churches were established in Eastern cities in an attempt to address the problems of each city.

---

† © 2014 The College Board.

B. SETTLEMENT HOUSES

1. The settlement house movement sought to provide support for the urban poor, particularly immigrants, by providing healthcare, job training, and daycare for children.

2. Jane Addams established the most successful program, Hull House, in Chicago, and had middle-class reformers live alongside the urban poor.

II. THE PROGRESSIVES

A. KEY POINTS OF PROGRESSIVISM

1. Progressives sought to use the government to help create a just society and ameliorate social problems.

2. Progressive leaders were primarily middle-class reformers concerned with urban and consumer issues.

3. Progressive reformers wanted to use governmental power to regulate industrial production and improve labor conditions.

4. Progressive reformers rejected Social Darwinism, arguing that cooperation, not competition, offered the best way to improve society.

B. KEY GOALS OF PROGRESSIVISM

1. Democratization of the political process

   ▸ Direct election of senators

   ▸ Women's suffrage

2. Reform of local governments

   ▸ Eliminate corruption at all levels of government

   ▸ The initiative, recall, and referendum were innovations that pushed local governments to become responsive to public opinion

   ▸ Commission or city-manager forms of government helped local officials become more professional

> ▶ Nonpartisan local governments led to the weakening of political machines

3. Regulation of big business

   ▶ Passage of child labor laws

   ▶ Passage of antitrust legislation

   ▶ Passage of the Pure Food and Drug Act

It is important to remember that Progressives, while seeking to reform government, were not socialists. While occasionally engaging in protests, they usually worked within the political system to accomplish their goals.

C. PROGRESSIVE CONSTITUTIONAL AMENDMENTS

1. The Sixteenth Amendment gave Congress the power to impose and collect income taxes.

2. The Seventeenth Amendment provided that senators be elected by popular vote (rather than by state legislatures).

3. The Eighteenth Amendment forbade the sale, manufacture, or transportation of intoxicating liquors.

4. The Nineteenth Amendment granted women the right to vote.

III. MUCKRAKERS

A. KEY POINTS

1. Muckrakers were investigative reporters who promoted social and political reforms by exposing corruption and urban problems.

2. Muckrakers were the leading critics of urban bosses and corporate robber barons.

3. The rise of mass-circulation newspapers and magazines enabled muckrakers to reach a large audience. The most influential muckraking magazine was *McClure's.*

B. LEADING MUCKRAKERS

1. Upton Sinclair

   ▶ Sinclair wrote the novel *The Jungle*, which graphically exposed abuses in the meatpacking industry.

   ▶ He helped convince Congress to pass the Meat Inspection Act of 1906 and the Pure Food and Drug Act of 1906.

2. Jacob Riis

   ▶ Riis was a journalist and photographer working primarily in New York City.

   ▶ Riis's book *How the Other Half Lives* provided poignant pictures that put a human face on the poverty and despair experienced by immigrants living in New York City's Lower East Side.

3. Ida Tarbell

   ▶ Tarbell was the foremost woman in the muckraking movement.

   ▶ She published a highly critical history of the Standard Oil Company, calling it the "Mother of Trusts."

4. Lincoln Steffens

   ▶ Steffens exposed corruption in urban political machines.

   ▶ His most famous exposé was "Shame of the Cities," published in *McClure's.*

It is important to be aware of several of the muckraking journalists. Tarbell is perhaps the most famous, but the others exercised considerable influence, including influence on President Theodore Roosevelt.

THE PROGRESSIVE PRESIDENTS

A. THEODORE ROOSEVELT (1901–1909)

1. Teddy Roosevelt was the most active advocate as president for the following Progressive issues:

   ▸ Conservation of natural resources and wildlife

   ▸ Ending unsanitary conditions in the meatpacking industry

   ▸ Reforming the railroad industry (He first did so by breaking a J.P. Morgan–led trust called Northern Securities using the Sherman Antitrust Act of 1890.)

   ▸ Eliminating unsafe drug products

   ▸ Eliminating (or reforming) trusts and monopolies

2. He promoted his Square Deal for labor by using arbitration to settle the Anthracite Coal Strike of 1902.

3. Roosevelt ran as the Progressive, or Bull Moose, candidate for president in the 1912 presidential election.

B. WILLIAM HOWARD TAFT (1909–1913)

1. Handpicked by Roosevelt to succeed him, Taft proved a major disappointment to the Progressives.

2. While contending that he supported lowered tariffs, Taft allowed passage of the Payne-Aldrich Tariff, which benefited manufacturers.

C. WOODROW WILSON (1913–1921)

1. Wilson was a vigorous reformer who launched an all-out assault on high tariffs, banking problems, and the trusts.

2. Wilson supported the Federal Reserve Act of 1913. The landmark act established a system of district banks coordinated by a central board. The new Federal Reserve System made currency and credit more elastic.

CONTENT REVIEW

83

Theodore Roosevelt, William Taft, and Woodrow Wilson all supported Progressive reforms. A thorough understanding of Progressivism requires familiarity with all three presidents.

V. FEMALE REFORMERS

A. THE FIGHT FOR SUFFRAGE

1. Frontier life tended to promote the acceptance of greater equality for women.

2. The only states with complete women's suffrage before 1900 were located west of the Mississippi. Wyoming (1869) was the first state to grant women the full right to vote.

3. The Nineteenth Amendment (1920) guaranteed women the right to vote.

B. WOMEN AND THE PROGRESSIVE REFORMS

1. Ida B. Wells-Barnett was an African American civil rights advocate and an early women's rights advocate. She is noted for her opposition to lynching.

2. Margaret Sanger advocated birth control and family planning, particularly among the urban poor; she founded Planned Parenthood.

3. Women reformers were also actively involved in the following Progressive Era reforms:

   ▶ Passage of child-labor legislation at the state level

   ▶ Campaigns to limit the working hours of women and children

C. WOMEN AND THE WORKPLACE

1. During the late nineteenth and early twentieth centuries, the majority of female workers employed outside the home were young and unmarried.

2. During the late nineteenth and early twentieth centuries, women were most likely to work outside the home as one of the following:

   ▶ Domestic servants

   ▶ Garment workers

   ▶ Teachers

   ▶ Cigar makers

3. During the late nineteenth century, women were least likely to work outside the home as either of these:

   ▶ Physicians

   ▶ Lawyers

 VI. **BLACK AMERICANS DURING THE PROGRESSIVE ERA, 1897–1917**

A. W.E.B. DU BOIS

1. During the Progressive Era, W.E.B. Du Bois emerged as the most influential advocate of full political, economic, and social equality for black Americans.

2. Du Bois helped found the National Association for the Advancement of Colored People (NAACP) in 1909.

3. Du Bois advocated the intellectual development of a "talented tenth" of the black population. Du Bois hoped that the talented tenth would become influential by, for example, continuing their education, writing books, or becoming directly involved in social change.

4. Du Bois opposed the implementation of Booker T. Washington's program for black progress. Du Bois supported cooperation with white people to further black progress. His goal was integration, not black separatism.

B. BOOKER T. WASHINGTON

1. Washington stressed that African Americans should not demand political equality but focus on economic opportunities.

2. In the Atlanta Compromise speech (1895), he advocated gradualism and patience on the path toward social equality.

C. THE NAACP

1. The NAACP rejected Booker T. Washington's gradualism and separatism.

2. The NAACP focused on using the courts to achieve equality and justice.

VII. AMERICAN IMPERIALISM: POLITICAL AND ECONOMIC EXPANSION

A. SOURCES OF AMERICAN IMPERIALISM

1. Sensational stories published by so-called yellow* journalists convinced many that the United States should intervene to protect Cubans from the Spanish.

2. The new Navy policy promoted by Alfred Thayer Mahan (*The Influence of Sea Power upon History)* and Theodore Roosevelt encouraged the United States to build a strong navy.

3. The United States witnessed European imperialism in Asia and Africa.

4. Social Darwinism, which emphasized survival of the fittest.

5. Unlike Manifest Destiny, imperialism included the idea of moral improvement by bringing the blessings of civilization to less technologically advanced people.

---

* sensationalist

B. SPANISH-AMERICAN WAR

1. Causes

   ▶ The U.S. battleship *Maine* was sunk mysteriously in Havana harbor, but imperialists blamed the Spanish.

   ▶ An escalating circulation battle between the "yellow journalism" newspapers of Joseph Pulitzer and William Randolph Hearst. Their sensational headlines and lurid stories aroused public support for a war to liberate Cuba from Spanish control.

2. Territorial Acquisitions

   ▶ As a result of the very brief Spanish-American War, Spain relinquished control of Puerto Rico, Cuba, Guam, and the Philippine Islands to the United States.

   ▶ By establishing a protectorate over Cuba and the Philippines, the United States began implementing an imperialist foreign policy.

3. The Debate over Annexing the Philippines

   ▶ The Anti-Imperialist League opposed annexation, arguing that it violated America's long-established commitment to the principles of self-determination and anticolonialism.

   ▶ Supporters of annexation argued that the United States had a moral responsibility to "civilize" the islands. They also pointed out that the Philippines could become a valuable trading partner.

   ▶ The United States provided troops and government assistance until the Japanese invaded in 1942.

C. THE ROOSEVELT COROLLARY TO THE MONROE DOCTRINE, 1904

1. President Theodore Roosevelt worried that the Dominican Republic and other Latin American nations could default on debts owed to European banks. These defaults might then provoke European military intervention.

2. Roosevelt issued the Roosevelt Corollary to the Monroe Doctrine to forestall European intervention.

3. The Roosevelt Corollary expanded America's role in Central America and the Caribbean by claiming America's right to assume the role of "an international police power." Presidents Roosevelt, Taft, and Wilson enforced the Roosevelt Corollary by sending U.S. troops to Cuba, Panama, Nicaragua, the Dominican Republic, Mexico, and Haiti. Roosevelt's foreign policy was known as big stick diplomacy.

4. Theodore Roosevelt explained and justified the Roosevelt Corollary as follows:

   > *"Chronic wrongdoing, or an impotence which results in a general loosening of the ties of civilized society, may in America, as elsewhere, ultimately require intervention by some civilized nation, and in the Western Hemisphere the adherence of the United States to the Monroe Doctrine may force the United States . . . to the exercise of an international police power."*

D. TAFT AND DOLLAR DIPLOMACY

1. President Taft believed he could use economic investments to bolster U.S. foreign policy.

2. Taft's attempt to use dollar diplomacy in Asia and Latin America achieved very little success.

E. THE OPEN DOOR POLICY

1. As China's Qing (Manchu) dynasty weakened, European powers carved out spheres of influence where they exercised political leverage and obtained exclusive commercial privileges.

2. Although he knew he could not force the Europeans to leave China, Secretary of State John Hay was determined to protect U.S. missionaries and commercial interests.

3. In 1899, Hay sent the Western nations with spheres of influence in China a note calling for open access to China for U.S. investment and commercial interests.

4. Known as the open door policy, it underscored America's commitment to free trade and its opposition to obstacles that thwarted international commerce.

5. The open door policy is easy to overlook, but it is an important part of American foreign policy. Be sure you know that this policy was intended to protect U.S. commercial interests in China.

VIII. THE ROAD TO WORLD WAR I

A. AMERICAN NEUTRALITY (1914–1917)

1. President Wilson sought to distance the United States from World War I by issuing a proclamation of neutrality, which was consistent with U.S. traditional policy developed under George Washington of avoiding European "entanglements."

2. Wilson insisted that all belligerents respect U.S. neutral rights on the high seas.

B. GERMANY'S CHALLENGE TO U.S. NEUTRALITY

1. Faced with a stalemate in the trenches across France and a British blockade that was exhausting its ability to continue fighting, Germany resumed a campaign of unrestricted submarine warfare in early February 1917 that affected U.S. shipping.

2. In late February 1917, German foreign secretary Arthur Zimmermann sent a secret telegram to the German minister in Mexico. Intercepted by British intelligence, the telegram asked Mexico to join a military alliance against the United States. In return, the Germans promised to help Mexico recover territories it had lost following the Mexican-American War.

C. WILSON'S WAR MESSAGE

1. Wilson accused the Germans of violating freedom of the seas, killing innocent Americans, and interfering with Mexico.

2. Wilson galvanized public opinion by calling on the United States to launch an idealistic crusade "to make the world safe for democracy."

IX. WORLD WAR I AT HOME AND ABROAD

A. THE GREAT MIGRATION

1. Causes of the migration:

    ▸ In 1915, the overwhelming majority of African Americans lived in the rural South.

    ▸ Jim Crow laws had denied African Americans their rights as citizens and forced them to endure poverty and systematic discrimination in the South.

    ▸ Beginning with World War I, the wartime demand for labor attracted African Americans to cities in the North and West.

B. THE COMMITTEE ON PUBLIC INFORMATION

1. The Committee on Public Information (also known as the Creel Committee, after its head, George Creel) used propaganda to arouse public support for the war and stifle dissent.

2. Americans were persuaded to buy war bonds and believed that Germany was a particularly barbarous nation.

3. Posters, many designed by George Montgomery Flagg, proved very persuasive as propaganda. ("Hate the Hun" became a popular catchphrase.)

X. TREATY OF VERSAILLES

A. THE FOURTEEN POINTS

1. Wilson issued a statement of Fourteen Points that included a call for the following:

    ▸ Open diplomacy

▸ Freedom of the seas

▸ The creation of an international organization (later called the League of Nations) to preserve the peace and security of its members

▸ National self-determination for oppressed minority groups

2. Wilson's Fourteen Points did not include the following:

▸ Recognition of Allied economic and territorial agreements made during the war

▸ A provision to create the International Monetary Fund

B. REASONS THE UNITED STATES DID NOT JOIN THE LEAGUE OF NATIONS

1. Wilson refused to compromise on the issue of America's unconditional adherence to the charter of the League of Nations; his stance hardened Senate opposition to the Treaty of Versailles.

2. Opponents (known as the Irreconcilables) believed that the League of Nations would lead to further involvement in foreign wars.

3. Senator Lodge was a skillful opponent of the League of Nations. The personal and political rivalry between Wilson and Lodge precluded any chance of a compromise, and the United States never ratified the Treaty of Versailles or joined the League of Nations.

XI. THE "RED SCARE" OF 1919–1920

A. THE BOLSHEVIK REVOLUTION IN RUSSIA

1. Led by Lenin, the Bolsheviks overthrew Tsar Nicholas II and seized power in Russia.

2. Widespread postwar labor strikes confused and frightened Americans.

CONTENT REVIEW

B. THE PALMER RAIDS OF 1919–1920

1. The Palmer Raids were caused by the fear of communism and radicalism.

2. These raids were conducted against suspected communists and anarchists. They were championed by Attorney General A. Mitchell Palmer.

3. The Palmer Raids disregarded basic civil liberties. For example, government agents in thirty-three cities broke into meeting halls and homes without search warrants. More than 4,000 people were jailed and denied counsel. They also deported suspected aliens without due process.

ECONOMIC CONDITIONS IN THE 1920s

A. SIGNS OF PROSPERITY

1. During the 1920s, the standard of living rose and cities grew in population.

2. All of the following provided evidence of economic prosperity during the 1920s:

   ▸ Larger numbers of women and men working in office jobs

   ▸ Increased emphasis on the marketing of consumer goods

   ▸ Growing investment in the stock market

3. The assembly-line production of Henry Ford's Model T enabled average U.S. families to purchase automobiles.

4. Beginning in 1920, the number of children aged ten to fifteen who were in the industrial workforce began to decline.

B. SIGNS OF TROUBLE

1. The least-prosperous group in the 1920s consisted of farmers in the Midwest and South.

2. For U.S. farmers, the years 1921 to 1929 were a period of falling prices for agricultural products. (For many farmers, the 1930s proved to be an even more difficult decade as a result of the Great Depression.)

 XIII. REPUBLICAN POLITICS: HARDING, COOLIDGE, AND HOOVER

A. REPUBLICAN PROSPERITY

1. Republican presidents of the 1920s favored tax cuts for wealthy Americans.

2. During the presidencies of Harding and Coolidge, the federal agencies created during the Progressive Era aided business.

B. FOREIGN POLICY

1. Despite its isolationist position in the 1920s, the U.S. government actively participated in decisions regarding international finance and the payment of war reparations.

2. The Washington Naval Conference of 1921–1922 was called to restrain the naval arms race among the United States, Britain, Japan, Italy, and France. The signatory nations agreed to specific limitations on the number of battleships each nation could build.

3. The Kellogg-Briand Pact of 1928 was an international agreement in which sixty-two nations pledged to foreswear war as an instrument of policy.

4. The United States responded to the economic crisis in Germany during the 1920s by adopting the Dawes Plan, which rescheduled German reparation payments and opened the way for American private loans to Germany. This plan, while achieving some initial success, failed during the Great Depression.

XIV. MODERNISM: ARTS AND MASS ENTERTAINMENT

A. THE ARTS

1. The "Lost Generation of the 1920s"

   ▸ Key writers included Sinclair Lewis and F. Scott Fitzgerald.

   ▸ They were called the Lost Generation because they grew disenchanted with U.S. society during the 1920s, causing many to move to Europe. They were also disillusioned by the horrors of World War I.

   ▸ Lost Generation writers criticized middle-class materialism and conformity. For example, Sinclair Lewis criticized middle-class life in novels such as *Babbitt* and *Main Street*.

The Lost Generation is an example of cultural history in the 1920s that you should know. The key point to remember is that writers such as F. Scott Fitzgerald and Sinclair Lewis criticized middle-class materialism and conformity and were disillusioned with traditional American values.

2. Jazz

   ▸ Black musicians such as Joseph ("Joe") King Oliver, W. C. Handy, and Jelly Roll Morton helped create jazz.

   ▸ Jazz was especially popular among the youth because it symbolized a desire to break from tradition.

B. MASS ENTERTAINMENT

1. Movies were the most popular form of mass entertainment.

2. Led by baseball, sports became a big business.

3. During the 1920s, technological innovations made long-distance radio broadcasting possible. National radio networks reached millions of Americans.

Note: Reflecting a shift away from Christian and patriotic values, sports figures and Hollywood entertainers began to replace political figures (such as Washington, Jefferson, and Lincoln) as heroes of the young during the 1920s.

 XV. RESPONSES TO MODERNISM: RELIGIOUS FUNDAMENTALISM AND NATIVISM

A. RELIGIOUS FUNDAMENTALISM

1. Fundamentalism was an antiliberal and antisecular Christian movement that gained strength throughout the 1920s.

2. Fundamentalism stressed a literal interpretation of the Bible, including the account of Creation in Genesis.

3. The Scopes Trial was an important test case.

   ▶ John T. Scopes was a high school biology teacher who, in 1925, was convicted of teaching evolution in his Dayton, Tennessee, classroom.

   ▶ The Scopes Trial illustrates the cultural conflict in the 1920s between fundamentalism and modernism.

   ▶ William Jennings Bryan assisted the prosecution, while Clarence Darrow defended Scopes.

   ▶ Although Scopes was convicted, he was only forced to pay a small fine of $100. In the end, the trial was more of a victory for secularism than it was for fundamentalism.

B. NATIVISM

1. The Ku Klux Klan (KKK)

   ▶ The 1920s witnessed a dramatic expansion of the KKK.

   ▶ D. W. Griffith's full-length film *The Birth of a Nation* glorified the KKK.

   ▶ During the 1920s, the KKK favored white supremacy and immigration restrictions.

▸ The KKK was hostile toward immigrants, Catholics, Jews, and African Americans.

The resurgence of the Ku Klux Klan during the 1920s provides a good example of the nativist reaction to modernism. Be sure you know the three times the KKK gained strength (1860s, 1920s, and 1960s). Also be sure you can identify D. W. Griffith's film **The Birth of a Nation,** *which was produced in 1915.*

2. The National Origins Act of 1924

▸ The primary purpose of the National Origins Act was to use quotas to restrict the flow of newcomers from southern and eastern Europe.

▸ These quotas were the primary reason for the decrease in the numbers of Europeans immigrating to the United States in the 1920s.

▸ The number of Mexicans and Puerto Ricans migrating to the United States increased because neither group was affected by the restrictive immigration acts of 1921 and 1924.

3. The Sacco and Vanzetti Case

▸ The Sacco and Vanzetti case was significant because it illustrated a fear of radicals and recent immigrants.

▸ Despite worldwide protests, the two immigrants were executed for the murder of a paymaster.

XVI. THE STRUGGLE FOR EQUALITY: AFRICAN AMERICANS AND WOMEN

A. AFRICAN AMERICANS

1. The Harlem Renaissance

▸ The Harlem Renaissance, an outpouring of black artistic and literary creativity, thrived during the 1920s, but only in the Harlem district of Manhattan.

> ▸ Harlem Renaissance writers and artists expressed pride in their African American culture. They supported full social and political equality for African Americans.

> ▸ Key figures in the Harlem Renaissance included James Weldon Johnson, Zora Neale Hurston, Langston Hughes, and Josephine Baker.

2. The Great Migration

> ▸ The migration of black Americans from the rural South to the urban North and West continued during the 1920s.

> ▸ The demand for industrial workers was the primary pull factor; the primary push factors came from the restrictions of Jim Crow segregation and the harsh reality of most sharecropping arrangements.

3. Marcus Garvey

> ▸ Marcus Garvey was the charismatic leader of the Universal Negro Improvement Association, which attracted a large following in the 1920s.

> ▸ Garveyism was identified with the following:

>> — *Black pride*

>> — *Black economic development*

>> — *Black nationalism*

>> — *Pan-Africanism*

> ▸ Garvey was committed to the idea that black Americans should return to Africa. His emphasis on black pride would be a key influence on certain African American leaders during the 1960s, including those who advocated Black Power.

B. WOMEN

1. Flappers

> ▸ Flappers symbolized the new freedom by challenging traditional U.S. attitudes toward women.

> ▸ Flappers favored short, bobbed hair; smoked cigarettes; and even wore the "new" one-piece bathing suits.

2. Women and the Workforce

> ▸ Although new jobs became available in offices and stores, the percentage of single women in the labor force actually declined between 1920 and 1930.

> ▸ Women did not receive equal pay and continued to face discrimination in the professions.

> ▸ Most married women did not seek employment outside the home.

3. Factors causing the decline of the feminist movement during the 1920s:

> ▸ Passage of the Nineteenth Amendment granting women the right to vote

> ▸ The inability of women's groups to agree on goals

> ▸ The decline of the Progressive reform movement

XVII. CAUSES OF THE GREAT DEPRESSION

A. CONSEQUENCES OF THE 1929 STOCK MARKET CRASH

1. A loss of confidence in the stock market.

2. A reduction in the output of manufactured goods.

3. A decline in investment in capital goods.

4. Between 1929 and 1932, unemployment rose from roughly 5 percent to 25 percent; the Dow Jones stock market index fell by close to 90 percent; and the gross national product (GNP) fell by almost 50 percent.

B. OVERPRODUCTION, UNDERCONSUMPTION, AND EXCESSIVE CONSUMER BORROWING

1. Companies overproduced consumer goods.

2. Consumers did not have enough money or credit to purchase goods.

3. Initially, loose lending standards by banks led to excessive consumer credit, including the ability to buy stocks on margin with as little as 10 percent down.

C. DECLINE IN FARM PROSPERITY

1. The decline in farm prosperity in the 1920s was an important factor contributing to the Great Depression in the 1930s.

2. Depression of the prices of agricultural products during the 1920s was an important sign of economic weakness. Farm prices fell by two-thirds from 1920 to 1930.

D. INTERNATIONAL TRADE

1. Serious dislocations in international trade were a significant cause of the Great Depression.

2. The Hawley-Smoot Tariff Act of 1930 raised tariffs, thus triggering a decline in trade. Within three years, world trade declined in value by 40 percent.

XVIII. HERBERT HOOVER AND THE GREAT DEPRESSION

A. HOOVER'S ECONOMIC POLICIES

1. President Hoover believed that the economic recovery of the United States depended primarily on the business community.

2. He approached the task of caring for unemployed workers by emphasizing the importance of private charities. He urged Americans to rely on the tradition of rugged individualism.

3. President Hoover supported federal loans to private businesses and to state and local governments.

4. He established the Reconstruction Finance Corporation (RFC) in a belated attempt to fight the Great Depression. This attempt proved to be too little, too late. Franklin Delano Roosevelt's (FDR's) administration later used the RFC much more aggressively.

B. THE BONUS EXPEDITIONARY FORCE

1. In 1932, a ragtag group of World War I veterans known as the Bonus Expeditionary Force marched on Washington, D.C. Their objective was to demand that Congress pay them a bonus, which had been promised to World War I veterans.

2. President Hoover authorized military force to disband the Bonus Expeditionary Force and destroy their encampment. This move proved to be a public relations nightmare, showing Hoover to be both callous and out of touch.

XIX. FRANKLIN D. ROOSEVELT AND THE NEW DEAL

A. GOALS

1. The three main themes of the New Deal were relief, recovery, and reform.

2. Unlike Hoover, FDR favored direct federal relief to individuals.

3. The New Deal was a reform program that sought to restructure U.S. capitalism rather than replace it with a socialist system.

4. After FDR adopted Keynesian economic theory, the New Deal eventually used deficit spending on public works programs to revive the economy.

B. THE FIRST HUNDRED DAYS

1. All of the following concerns were addressed during the first hundred days of the New Deal in 1933:

   ▸ Restoring public confidence in the banking system

▸ Creating new jobs in the public sector to reduce unemployment

▸ Raising farm prices by restricting agricultural production

▸ Providing mortgage support for homeowners

▸ Creating the Tennessee Valley Authority as a model project to provide cheap electricity, prevent floods, and serve as an experiment in regional planning

2. All of the following were created during the first hundred days of the New Deal:

▸ The Civilian Conservation Corps

▸ The National Recovery Administration

▸ The Agricultural Adjustment Act

▸ The Tennessee Valley Authority

C. FARM POLICY: THE AGRICULTURAL ADJUSTMENT ACT OF 1933

1. The purpose of the Agricultural Adjustment Act (AAA) of 1933 was to raise farm prices by limiting agricultural production.

2. The AAA established a national system of crop controls and offered subsidies to farmers who agreed to limit the production of specific crops.

3. Hungry Americans were outraged when farmers plowed crops under and destroyed millions of piglets in an attempt to boost farm prices.

D. THE NATIONAL INDUSTRIAL RECOVERY ACT

1. The National Industrial Recovery Act (NIRA) sought to combat the Great Depression by fostering government–business cooperation.

2. The NIRA allowed businesses to regulate themselves through codes of fair competition.

3. The NIRA was relatively unsuccessful, unlike Social Security, which proved to be much more enduring.

Note: Both the AAA and the NIRA were declared unconstitutional by the Supreme Court, which caused FDR to engage in what became known as his court-packing scheme in 1937. This court-packing scheme was ultimately unsuccessful.

E. THE CIVILIAN CONSERVATION CORPS

1. The Civilian Conservation Corps (CCC) was created during the first hundred days of the New Deal.

2. It employed young men in rural work projects, thus reducing urban unemployment.

F. THE SOCIAL SECURITY ACT OF 1935

1. The Social Security Act created a federal pension system funded by taxes on a worker's wages and by an equivalent contribution by employers.

2. Since the 1970s, the aging of the U.S. population has been widely seen as a threat to the long-term viability of the Social Security system.

G. THE WAGNER ACT OF 1935

1. The Wagner Act, also known as the National Labor Relations Act, is often called the Magna Carta of labor because it ensured workers' rights to organize and bargain collectively.

2. It led to a dramatic increase in labor union membership.

H. THE NEW DEAL AND AFRICAN AMERICANS

1. To a limited extent, New Deal programs helped African Americans survive some of the worst hardships of the Great Depression.

2. The New Deal did not directly confront racial segregation and injustice. As a result, there was no major action on civil rights.

3. African Americans joined the Democratic Party in large numbers because of the popularity of New Deal programs.

I. THE COURT-PACKING SCHEME

1. The Supreme Court declared key parts of the New Deal unconstitutional, undermining several significant programs.

2. FDR responded by attempting to "pack" (add more justices to) the Supreme Court. His goal was to make sure that New Deal laws would be found constitutional. Although this plan initially failed, several conservative judges retired; FDR did not suffer any more defeats at the hands of the Supreme Court in relation to his New Deal programs.

J. IMPACT OF THE NEW DEAL

1. Historians generally regard the New Deal as a program of reform rather than of revolution because the New Deal sought to restructure U.S. capitalism rather than replace it.

2. The New Deal did mark a new direction for the federal government. For example, New Deal programs all demonstrated a willingness to use the government to enhance social welfare. As part of this process, FDR also significantly expanded the role of the presidency.

3. The New Deal programs were partially successful in reducing unemployment and reviving the economy.

4. The New Deal led to the emergence of the Democratic Party as the majority party.

5. The New Deal helped African Americans survive the Great Depression.

6. It is important to remember that the United States did not fully emerge from the Great Depression until the massive military expenditures prompted by World War II.

7. Key goals that the New Deal did *not* achieve include the following:

   ▶ The New Deal did not integrate the armed forces.

▶ The New Deal did not include programs specifically designed to protect the civil liberties of African Americans.

▶ The New Deal did not nationalize basic industries.

▶ The New Deal did not end the Great Depression.

Be sure you have a solid understanding of the causes of the Great Depression and the purposes and programs of the New Deal. It represents a tremendous increase in the size and scope of the federal government in dealing with social issues.

XX. LABOR AND UNION RECOGNITION

A. THE CIO AND JOHN L. LEWIS

1. The CIO (Congress of Industrial Organizations) organized unskilled and semiskilled factory workers in basic manufacturing industries such as steel and automobiles.

2. John L. Lewis explained the goals and strategy of the CIO in this manner:

   "The productive methods and facilities of modern industry have been completely transformed. . . . Skilled artisans make up only a small proportion of the workers. Obviously the bargaining strength of employees under these conditions no longer rests in organizations of skilled craftsmen. It is dependent upon a national union representing all employees—whether skilled or unskilled, or whether working by brain or brawn—in each basic industry."

B. THE SPLIT BETWEEN THE AFL AND THE CIO

1. The American Federation of Labor (AFL) split apart at its national convention in 1935.

2. A majority of AFL leaders refused to grant charters to new unions that were organized on an industry-wide basis.

3. The AFL favored the organization of workers according to their skills and trades, while the CIO favored the organization of all workers in a particular industry.

XXI. THE NEW DEAL COALITION

A. THE DEMOCRATIC COALITION

1. All of the following were part of the Democratic coalition that elected FDR in 1936:

   ▸ White southerners

   ▸ African Americans

   ▸ Ethnic minorities

   ▸ Union members

2. The Democratic coalition did *not* include wealthy industrialists.

B. SHIFT IN VOTING

1. As a result of the Emancipation Proclamation and the Reconstruction amendments, African Americans were loyal voters for the Republican Party until the 1930s.

2. During the presidency of Franklin D. Roosevelt, large numbers of African American voters switched their allegiance from the Republican Party to the Democratic Party.

3. Although the New Deal was popular for many, it did have a number of outspoken critics. For example, Dr. Francis E. Townsend, Huey Long, and Father Charles Coughlin all criticized aspects of the New Deal.

CONTENT REVIEW

XXII. AMERICAN SOCIETY DURING THE NEW DEAL

A. HOOVERVILLES

1. Millions of Americans were evicted from their homes and apartments because they could not pay their mortgages or their rent.

2. Hoovervilles (shantytowns of unemployed and homeless people) sprang up in most U.S. cities.

B. PEOPLE ON THE MOVE

1. During the 1930s, the Great Depression led to a mass migration of Americans looking for work.

2. African Americans continued to migrate from small Southern towns to urban centers in the North and West.

XXIII. AMERICAN RESPONSES TO THE GROWING THREAT OF WAR

A. THE STIMSON DOCTRINE, 1932

1. In September 1931, the Japanese invaded and conquered the Chinese province of Manchuria.

2. The Stimson Doctrine (1932) declared that the United States would not recognize any territorial acquisitions achieved by force. Although the United States did not recognize the Japanese occupation, the Hoover administration refrained from taking any military action.

3. The failure of the United States and other powers to take any concrete action marked the failure of collective security (the League of Nations was designed to ensure that such a failure did not happen).

B. THE NEUTRALITY ACTS

1. A series of Neutrality Acts in the 1930s were expressions of a commitment to isolationism.

2. During the 1930s, isolationists drew support for their position from Washington's Farewell Address and disillusionment with U.S. involvement in World War I.

C. THE LEND-LEASE PROGRAM

1. Under the lend-lease program, President Roosevelt authorized the sale of surplus military equipment to the Allies while officially remaining neutral.

2. Lend-lease was used primarily to help Great Britain and the Soviet Union resist Nazi Germany.

XXIV. THE ATTACK ON PEARL HARBOR AND THE GERMANY-FIRST STRATEGY

A. PEARL HARBOR

1. The Japanese war machine was dependent on shipments of oil, aviation gasoline, steel, and scrap iron from the United States. In late 1940, the Roosevelt administration imposed the first of a series of embargoes on Japan-bound supplies. In mid-1941, President Franklin D. Roosevelt froze Japanese assets in the United States and halted all shipments of gasoline.

2. The U.S. actions left Japanese leaders with two alternatives: (1) they could give in to American demands that they withdraw from Manchuria or (2) they could thwart the embargo by attacking the U.S. fleet at Pearl Harbor and then seizing the oil supplies and other raw materials in Southeast Asia.

3. The Japanese attack on Pearl Harbor occurred after diplomatic negotiations with the United States had reached a stalemate.

Pearl Harbor is the only World War II battle that has appeared on past APUSH exams. It is unlikely you will see the Battle of the Bulge, the D-Day invasion, or other battles appear as test questions so don't spend time memorizing them. Focus on the causes and results of World War II.

B. GERMANY FIRST

1. The Japanese attack on December 7, 1941, unified the United States. Angry Americans vowed to avenge the treacherous attack on Pearl Harbor.

2. After the attack on Pearl Harbor, the United States announced a strategy of first defeating Germany and then turning to a full-scale attack on Japan. Although at first unpopular, the get-Germany-first strategy prevailed. The United States could not allow Hitler to defeat Great Britain and the Soviet Union, thus transforming the continent into an unconquerable Fortress Europe.

XXV. DIPLOMACY AND THE BIG THREE

A. LATIN AMERICA

1. Based on the principles of the Good Neighbor Policy, the Roosevelt administration formally renounced the right to intervene in Latin America.

2. During World War II, the United States sought greater cooperation with the nations of Latin America, primarily to develop a hemispheric common front against fascism.

B. THE PHILIPPINE ISLANDS

1. In response to widespread anti-imperialist sentiments, the United States pledged to grant independence to the Philippine Islands following the Spanish-American War, but the United States then decided to maintain a certain level of control until FDR decided to change course.

2. The Philippines were conquered by the Japanese in 1942 and gained independence from the United States in 1946.

C. THE BIG THREE

1. The Big Three were Franklin Roosevelt, Winston Churchill, and Josef Stalin.

2. They demanded the unconditional surrender of Germany and Japan.

3. The Big Three attended several conferences and held their final meeting at Yalta in February 1945.

4. At Yalta, Stalin promised free elections for Poland and Eastern Europe and to join the fight against Japan following the defeat of Germany. (Stalin later reneged on his promise of free elections, causing friction with the United States and leading to the start of the Cold War.)

 ## XXVI. WARTIME MOBILIZATION OF THE ECONOMY

A. IMPACT OF MILITARY SPENDING

1. Military spending revived the U.S. economy and virtually ended unemployment.

2. The dramatic increase in military spending enabled the United States to finally emerge from the Great Depression as the nation went back to work.

B. PRICE CONTROLS

1. The government instituted direct price controls to halt inflation.

2. The Office of Price Administration (OPA) established a nationwide rationing system for consumer goods such as coffee and gasoline.

 ## XXVII. AFRICAN AMERICANS AND WOMEN

A. AFRICAN AMERICANS

1. The war years witnessed the continuing migration of African Americans from the rural South to urban centers in the North and West. All told, some 1.6 million African Americans left the South.

2. President Roosevelt issued an executive order forbidding discrimination in defense industries. The order was monitored by the Fair Employment Practices Commission.

B. WOMEN AND THE WORKPLACE

1. "Rosie the Riveter" (after a "We Can Do It!" poster by J. Howard Miller) was a nickname given during World War II to American women who did industrial work in the 1940s.

2. The war mobilization caused a significant movement of married women into the workforce.

Although you should not expect to find questions about battles and generals, you should prepare for questions about developments on the home front, particularly related to industrial production and limitations on civil liberties.

XXVIII. CIVIL LIBERTIES AND CIVIL RIGHTS DURING WARTIME

A. THE INTERNMENT OF JAPANESE AMERICANS

1. In March 1942, President Roosevelt ordered that all Japanese Americans living on the West Coast be removed to relocation centers for the duration of the war.

2. Japanese Americans were sent to the internment camps on the grounds that they constituted a potential security threat.

B. *KOREMATSU v. UNITED STATES*

1. The relocation of Japanese Americans during World War II raised the constitutionality of their internment as a wartime necessity.

2. The Supreme Court ruling in *Korematsu v. United States* upheld the constitutionality of the internment of Japanese Americans as a wartime necessity.

XXIX. THE UNITED STATES AND THE ATOMIC BOMB

A. MANHATTAN PROJECT

1. President Roosevelt authorized the Manhattan Project, which brought top American scientists to Los Alamos, New Mexico, to develop the atomic bomb.

2. President Truman authorized the use of the atomic bomb on the Japanese cities of Hiroshima and Nagasaki.

3. The United States was the only country that possessed atomic bombs in 1945.

B. TRUMAN'S REASONING FOR USING THE ATOMIC BOMB

1. Continuing to use conventional weapons and tactics would result in the loss of thousands of American lives if a land invasion of Japan were required.

2. Using the atomic bomb would persuade the Japanese to surrender.

3. Ending the war against Japan as quickly as possible would prevent Soviet intervention.

4. Using the atomic bomb would convince the Soviet Union of the need to be more cooperative in formulating its postwar plans.

PERID 8
1945–1980

Key Concepts[†]

Concept 1: The United States responded to an uncertain and unstable postwar world by asserting and attempting to defend a position of global leadership, with far-reaching domestic and international consequences.

Concept 2: Liberalism, based on anticommunism abroad and a firm belief in the efficacy of governmental, and especially federal, power to achieve social goals at home, reached its apex in the mid-1960s and generated a variety of political and cultural responses.

Concept 3: Postwar economic, demographic, and technological changes had a far-reaching impact on U.S. society, politics, and the environment.

I. TRUMAN AND CONTAINMENT

A. KEY POINTS

1. Containment was the foreign policy plan utilized by the United States to contain or block Soviet expansion.

2. Containment was the primary U.S. foreign policy from the announcement of the Truman Doctrine in 1947 to the fall of the Berlin Wall in 1989.

B. ROLE OF GEORGE KENNAN

1. George Kennan was a U.S. diplomat and specialist on the Soviet Union.

[†] © 2014 The College Board.

2. Kennan wrote an influential article (the so-called Long Telegram) advocating that the United States focus its foreign policy on containing the spread of Soviet influence.

When you think about the concept of containment, you probably think of the Truman Doctrine, the Marshall Plan, and NATO. Don't overlook George Kennan. His widely circulated Long Telegram played a key role in persuading the Truman administration to adopt the policy of containment.

C. THE TRUMAN DOCTRINE

1. President Truman was determined to block the expansion of Soviet influence into Greece and Turkey.

2. On March 12, 1947, Truman asked Congress for $400 million in economic aid for Greece and Turkey.

3. Truman justified the aid by declaring that the United States would support "free peoples who are resisting attempted subjugations by armed minorities or by outside pressures." This sweeping pledge became known as the Truman Doctrine.

D. THE MARSHALL PLAN

1. World War II left Western Europe devastated and vulnerable to Soviet influence.

2. The Marshall Plan was a program of massive economic aid designed to promote the recovery of war-torn Europe and, at the same time, prevent the spread of communist influence.

3. The Marshall Plan was an integral part of Truman's policy of containment. Here is an excerpt from Truman's speech justifying the Marshall Plan:

> "Our policy is directed not against any country or doctrine, but against hunger, poverty, desperation, and chaos. Its purpose should be the revival of a working economy in the world so as to permit the emergence of political and social conditions in which free institutions can exist. . . . Any

> *government that is willing to assist in the task of recovery*
> *will find full cooperation, I am sure, on the part of the*
> *United States government."*

4. The Marshall Plan was effective in both of its goals: Western Europe's economies (particularly Germany's) recovered, and communism made few inroads.

E. THE NATO ALLIANCE

1. Ten Western European nations joined with the United States and Canada to form a defensive military alliance called the North Atlantic Treaty Organization (NATO).

2. The NATO alliance marked a decisive break from America's tradition of isolationism and somewhat of a rejection of the model established by Washington and Jefferson of avoiding entangling alliances.

F. THE BERLIN AIRLIFT (1948)

1. Fearing a resurgent Germany, the Soviet Union cut off Western land access to West Berlin, located deep within the Soviet zone.

2. President Truman ordered a massive airlift of food, fuel, and other supplies to the beleaguered citizens of West Berlin.

3. The Berlin Airlift marked a crucial and successful test of containment as the Soviets backed down and allowed open access to West Berlin.

II. THE COLD WAR IN ASIA: CHINA, KOREA, AND VIETNAM

A. THE "FALL" OF CHINA (1949)

1. Led by Mao Zedong, the Chinese Communists defeated the Chinese Nationalists after a long struggle and declared the People's Republic of China both an independent and a Communist nation.

CONTENT REVIEW

2. The collapse of Nationalist China was viewed as a devastating defeat for the United States and its Cold War allies. The "fall" of China had the following consequences:

   ▸ The United States refused to recognize the new government in Beijing.

   ▸ The United States interpreted the Chinese Revolution as part of a menacing Communist monolith under Moscow's command.

   ▸ The "fall" of China contributed to the anti-Communist hysteria in the United States.

B. THE KOREAN WAR

1. The United Nations and Korea

   ▸ The Korean War began when North Korea invaded South Korea on June 25, 1950.

   ▸ President Truman took advantage of a temporary Soviet absence from the United Nations Security Council to obtain a unanimous condemnation of North Korea as an aggressor. The Korean War thus marked the first collective military action by the United Nations.

   ▸ It is important to note that the Korean War was fought under UN auspices, with 90% of the troops being American. In contrast, the Vietnam War was not fought under UN auspices.

2. A Limited War

   ▸ The Korean War was a limited war that extended the containment policy to Asia.

   ▸ Stung by criticism that the Democratic Party had "lost" China, Truman was determined to defend South Korea.

3. Truman's Firing of MacArthur

   ▸ The Chinese entered the war when UN forces approached the strategic Yalu River.

▶ General MacArthur disagreed with President Truman's policy of fighting a limited war. MacArthur publicly favored a blockade of the Chinese coast and bombardment of Chinese bases. Truman responded by relieving MacArthur of his command for insubordination.

4. Peace Agreement

▶ The combatants finally signed an armistice in July 1953, although the war never officially ended.

▶ The armistice set the border between North Korea and South Korea near the 38th parallel at approximately the prewar boundary.

5. Truman's Integration of the Armed Forces

▶ Prior to the Korean War, African Americans fought in segregated units.

▶ President Truman ordered the racial desegregation of the armed forces. The Korean War marked the first time U.S. forces had fought in integrated units.

Test Tip

President Truman's decision to desegregate the armed forces marked an important, but often overlooked, event. This is an important milestone in the civil rights movement, which is rarely cited in textbooks.

C. THE VIETNAM WAR, 1946–1963

1. Containment and Vietnam

▶ Following World War II, the United States adopted a policy of containment to halt the expansion of Communist influence.

▶ American involvement in Vietnam grew out of the policy commitments and assumptions of containment.

2. The French Withdrawal

▸ Following World War II, the French continued to exercise influence and control over French Indochina.

▸ Led by Ho Chi Minh, the Viet Minh defeated the French at the pivotal battle of Dien Bien Phu. Following their defeat, the French withdrew from Vietnam in 1954.

▸ The United States refused to sign the Geneva Accords and soon replaced France as the dominant Western power in Indochina.

3. The Domino Effect

▸ U.S. foreign policy planners believed that if one nation fell under Communist control, nearby nations would inevitably also fall under Communist influence (the domino effect).

▸ Here is how then-Secretary of State Dean Rusk explained the domino effect: "If Indo-China were to fall and if its fall led to the loss of all of Southeast Asia, then the United States might eventually be forced back to Hawaii, as it was before the Second World War."

 ## III. KEY COLD WAR EVENTS DURING THE EISENHOWER ADMINISTRATION

A. *SPUTNIK*

1. Launched by the Soviet Union in 1957, *Sputnik* was the first Earth-orbiting satellite.

2. *Sputnik* stunned the United States, prompting President Eisenhower to establish the National Aeronautics and Space Administration (NASA).

3. *Sputnik* made education an issue of national security. Congress responded by passing the National Defense Education Act, which significantly expanded federal aid to education by funding programs in mathematics, foreign languages, and the sciences.

B. DIPLOMATIC CRISES

1. Egypt seized the Suez Canal (1956).

2. Castro gained control over Cuba (1959).

3. The Soviet Union shot down a U.S. U-2 spy plane (1960).

The Suez crisis, the rise of Castro, and the U-2 crisis were all very important foreign policy events during the Eisenhower administration and reflected the unstable world situation during the Cold War.

IV. THE RISE AND FALL OF McCARTHYISM

A. BACKGROUND

1. Joseph McCarthy, a relatively unknown U.S. senator from Wisconsin, catapulted to national attention by making sensational accusations that the U.S. State Department was "thoroughly infested with Communists."

2. "McCarthyism" refers to the period during the early 1950s when Senator McCarthy made public accusations of disloyalty without sufficient evidence.

B. THE RISE OF McCARTHYISM

1. The following factors contributed to the rise of McCarthyism:

   ▶ Fears raised by the "fall" of China to Communism and the emergence of Mao Zedong as the leader of the People's Republic of China

▸ Fears raised by the Soviet Union's development of an atomic bomb in 1949, the same year that China fell to the Communists

▸ Fears raised by President Truman's emphasis on a foreign policy designed to contain Soviet expansion

▸ Fears raised by revelations that Soviet spies had infiltrated sensitive agencies and programs in the United States. Two spy cases seemed to add credibility to the fear:

— *The first case involved a former State Department official named Alger Hiss who was accused of passing secrets to the Soviet Union. Young California Congressman Richard Nixon played a key and highly publicized role in the investigation of Hiss.*

— *The second case involved Ethel and Julius Rosenberg. The Rosenbergs were executed for secretly giving information to the Soviet Union about the U.S. atomic bomb project.*

C. McCARTHY'S TACTICS

1. McCarthy directed his attack at alleged Communists and Communist sympathizers.

2. Senator McCarthy played on the fears of Americans that Communists had infiltrated the State Department and other federal agencies.

3. McCarthy's accusations helped create a climate of paranoia, and Americans became preoccupied with the perceived threat posed by the spread of Communism.

4. As a result of McCarthy's anti-Communist witch-hunt, millions of Americans were forced to take loyalty oaths and undergo loyalty investigations.

5. The fear of Communist infiltration spread to the motion picture industry. Hollywood executives instituted a blacklist of about 500 entertainment professionals who were denied employment because of their real or imagined political beliefs or associations. The blacklist ruined the careers of many actors, writers, and directors.

6. Senator McCarthy and others, many of whom were members of the House Un-American Activities Committee, cynically used the climate of fear for their own political advantage.

7. Because of McCarthy's aggressive style, others feared opposing him because they would be accused of fostering Communism.

D. THE FALL OF McCARTHY

1. In 1954, Senator McCarthy accused the U.S. Army of being infiltrated by Communist sympathizers after he discovered the promotion of an army dentist who had once been a communist.

2. A huge national audience watched the Army-McCarthy hearings. McCarthy's boorish conduct and lack of evidence turned public opinion against him. A few months later, the Senate formally condemned him for "conduct unbecoming a member."

3. McCarthy died three years later of chronic alcoholism.

The rise and fall of Senator Joseph McCarthy is key to understanding the culture of the 1950s. Make sure that you review and study the key points listed above in the review of McCarthyism. Also, note that both Richard Nixon and John F. Kennedy began their political careers as outspoken opponents of Communism.

V. MILESTONES IN THE MODERN CIVIL RIGHTS MOVEMENT

A. PRESIDENT HARRY S. TRUMAN

1. President Truman issued an executive order desegregating the armed forces in 1948, the most significant civil rights breakthrough of his administration.

2. A group of Southern conservatives called the Dixiecrats walked out of the 1948 Democratic National Convention to demonstrate their opposition to President Truman's civil rights legislation.

B. *BROWN v. BOARD OF EDUCATION OF TOPEKA,* 1954

1. The Supreme Court ruled that segregation in public schools was a denial of the equal protection of the laws guaranteed in the Fourteenth Amendment.

2. The Supreme Court decision directly contradicted the legal principle of "separate but equal" established by *Plessy v. Ferguson* in 1896.

3. As a result of its victory in *Brown v. Board of Education of Topeka,* the National Association for the Advancement of Colored People (NAACP) continued to base its court suits on the Equal Protection Clause of the Fourteenth Amendment.

C. PRESIDENT DWIGHT D. EISENHOWER

1. President Eisenhower sent federal troops to Little Rock's Central High School to enforce court-ordered desegregation.

2. Eisenhower supported his decision by saying, "The very basis of our individual rights and freedoms rests upon the certainty that the President and the Executive Branch of Government will support and insure the carrying out of the decisions of the Federal courts, even, when necessary, with all the means at the President's command."

3. Although he did send troops to Little Rock, Eisenhower was not a vigorous supporter of civil rights legislation.

4. The primary power granted to the Civil Rights Commission in 1957 was the authority to investigate and report on cases involving discrimination. Overall, it proved to be a weak piece of legislation that did little to help African Americans.

D. DR. MARTIN LUTHER KING, JR.

1. Dr. King's goal was integration of the races in all areas of society through nonviolent pressure and resistance.

2. Dr. King's theory of nonviolent civil disobedience was influenced by the writings of Henry David Thoreau and the practices of Mahatma Gandhi.

3. Dr. King was head of the Southern Christian Leadership Conference (SCLC).

4. On December 1, 1955, Rosa Parks refused to give up her bus seat to a white passenger. Her refusal helped galvanize the Montgomery Bus Boycott led by Dr. King.

5. The following quotation vividly expresses Dr. King's philosophy of nonviolence:

   "The problem with hatred and violence is that they intensify the fears of the white majority, and leave them less ashamed of their prejudices toward Negroes. In the guilt and confusion confronting our society, violence only adds to chaos. It deepens the brutality of the oppressor and increases the bitterness of the oppressed. Violence is the antithesis of creativity and wholeness. It destroys community and makes brotherhood impossible."

Test Tip

While Dr. Martin Luther King, Jr. was the most prominent civil rights leader, other leaders, such as Malcolm X and Stokely Carmichael, were also influential. They did not, however, support Dr. King's nonviolent approach. Be sure to review the key events and characters of the U.S. civil rights movement.

CONTENT REVIEW

E. THE SIT-IN MOVEMENT

1. Students staged the first sit-ins at a lunch counter in Greensboro, North Carolina, in 1960 to protest segregation in public facilities.

2. The sit-ins provide an excellent example of nonviolent civil disobedience.

VI. PROSPERITY AND CHANGE

A. THE AFFLUENT SOCIETY

1. The decade after World War II was characterized by the following:

   ▸ Unprecedented prosperity

   ▸ A population explosion known as the baby boom

   ▸ Rapid and extensive suburbanization

B. WOMEN AND THE WORKPLACE

1. Following World War II, large numbers of women left their industrial jobs to make room for returning soldiers.

2. As Rosie the Riveter gave up her tools and returned home, the housewife became the new ideal for married women.

3. Television programs such as *I Love Lucy*, *Father Knows Best*, and *The Honeymooners* all portrayed women in their roles as loyal and subservient housewives.

C. INTERSTATE HIGHWAYS AND THE GROWTH OF SUBURBIA

1. Passed during the Eisenhower administration, the Federal Highway Act of 1956 created the interstate highway system.

2. The Federal Highway Act of 1956 vastly accelerated the growth of suburbia and promoted the car culture.

VII. SOCIAL CRITICS, NONCONFORMISTS, AND CULTURAL REBELS

A. SOCIAL CRITICS

1. Social commentators criticized the conformity of postwar culture. The leading social critics were:

   ▶ William H. Whyte—*The Organization Man*

   ▶ David Riesman—*The Lonely Crowd*

   ▶ John Kenneth Galbraith—*The Affluent Society*

2. Critics lambasted most television programs, calling the new medium, as Federal Communications Commission head Newton Minow put it, a "vast wasteland."

B. NONCONFORMISTS

1. Led by Jack Kerouac, Beat Generation writers rejected middle-class culture and conformity.

2. In his book *On the Road*, Kerouac expressed the alienation and disillusionment he felt toward mainstream U.S. culture.

The 1920s and 1950s were similar decades. Both followed devastating world wars. Both featured anticommunist crusades. In addition, both the Lost Generation writers of the 1920s and the Beat Generation writers of the 1950s wrote about their alienation and disillusionment with U.S. conformity and materialism.

C. CULTURAL REBELS

1. Rock 'n' Roll

   ▶ Rock 'n' roll first emerged during the 1950s.

   ▶ Rock 'n' roll was inspired and strongly influenced by African American musical traditions, especially rhythm and blues.

   ▶ Elvis Presley was the most popular rock 'n' roll musician of his era.

CONTENT REVIEW

2. Abstract Expressionist Artists

▸ Abstract expressionism emerged in New York City in the late 1940s and early 1950s.

▸ Led by Jackson Pollock, abstract expressionist artists abandoned painting methods that represented reality. Instead, they created works of art that expressed their state of mind.

3. Movie Stars

▸ Movie stars such as James Dean and Marlon Brando symbolized youthful rebellion.

VIII. THE NEW FRONTIER AND THE GREAT SOCIETY

A. THE NEW FRONTIER

1. The Election of 1960

▸ John F. Kennedy (JFK) was a Roman Catholic— the first to be nominated since Al Smith's losing campaign in 1928.

▸ The 1960 election was the first to include televised debates. Audiences estimated at 60 million or more watched each of the four debates between JFK and Richard Nixon.

2. Camelot

▸ JFK was the youngest elected president in U.S. history.

▸ JFK challenged Americans to boldly enter the "New Frontier" of the 1960s.

▸ Kennedy and his glamorous wife, Jacqueline, presided over an elegant White House that was soon nicknamed Camelot after the legendary court of King Arthur.

> ▶ In his inaugural address, JFK challenged Americans: "Ask not what your country can do for you, ask what you can do for your country."

B. JFK'S ASSASSINATION

1. While on a visit to Dallas, Texas, JFK was shot and killed on November 22, 1963. Vice president Lyndon B. Johnson was sworn in as president.

2. JFK's assassin, Lee Harvey Oswald, was shot two days later, leading to conspiracy theories regarding who ordered JFK's killing.

3. A commission headed by Chief Justice Earl Warren concluded that Oswald acted alone.

C. THE GREAT SOCIETY OF LYNDON JOHNSON

1. Primary Goals

   > ▶ Use the federal government to enhance social welfare.

   > ▶ Use education and job training to help disadvantaged people overcome the cycle of poverty limiting their opportunities.

2. Legislative Achievements

   > ▶ Civil Rights Act of 1964

   > ▶ Voting Rights Act of 1965

   > ▶ Medicare and Medicaid

   > ▶ War on Poverty

   > ▶ Programs offering significant federal aid to education, including Head Start

3. Similarities Between the New Deal and the Great Society

   > ▶ Both the New Deal and the Great Society used the government to enhance social welfare.

▶ Both the New Deal and the Great Society included all of the following:

— *Government-sponsored employment programs*

— *Federal programs to encourage housing construction*

— *Federal legislation to help the elderly*

4. Differences Between the New Deal and the Great Society

▶ Preschool education for disadvantaged children was an innovative Great Society program that was not an extension of a New Deal program.

▶ In contrast to the New Deal, the Great Society included federal legislation protecting the civil liberties of African Americans.

It is important to know the similarities and differences between the New Deal and the Great Society. Both represent the largest governmental social program expansions in U.S. history. Especially note that, unlike the New Deal, the Great Society included landmark laws that protected the civil liberties and voting rights of African Americans.

IX. 1960s CIVIL RIGHTS MOVEMENTS

A. THE CIVIL RIGHTS MOVEMENT

1. Leadership of Dr. Martin Luther King, Jr.

▶ In April 1963, Dr. King led a campaign against segregation in Birmingham, Alabama.

▶ Within a few days, Police Commissioner Eugene "Bull" Connor arrested Dr. King and other marchers. In his "Letter from Birmingham Jail," Dr. King argued that citizens have "a moral responsibility to disobey unjust laws." Dr. King believed that civil disobedience is justified in the face of unjust laws.

▶ Connor ordered his police to use attack dogs and high-pressure fire hoses to disperse civil rights marchers. Millions of horrified TV viewers watched what Dr. King called a "visual demonstration of sin."

▶ Outraged by the violence, President Kennedy called on Congress to pass a comprehensive civil rights bill that would end legal discrimination on the basis of race.

▶ In August 1963, Dr. King led a massive march on Washington to support President Kennedy's bill. Appealing for racial harmony and social justice, Dr. King declared, "I have a dream that my four little children will one day live in a nation where they will not be judged by the color of their skin, but by the content of their character."

▶ On July 2, 1964, President Johnson signed the Civil Rights Act of 1964. This landmark legislation prohibited discrimination because of race, religion, national origin, or gender. The act banned racial discrimination in private facilities such as restaurants and theaters that are open to the public.

2. Voter Registration Drives

▶ Freedom Riders worked throughout the South to register African American voters.

▶ They were often met with violence by the Ku Klux Klan and police officials.

3. Black Power

▶ The Black Power movement of the late 1960s advocated that African Americans establish control of their political and economic lives.

▶ The most important Black Power leaders were Malcolm X, at one time the spokesman of the Nation of Islam; Stokely Carmichael, head of the Student Nonviolent Coordinating Committee (SNCC); and Huey Newton, head of the Black Panthers.

B. THE WOMEN'S RIGHTS MOVEMENT

1. Betty Friedan

   ▸ Betty Friedan was the author of *The Feminine Mystique* and the first president of the National Organization for Women (NOW).

   ▸ NOW was founded in 1966 in order to challenge sex discrimination in the workplace.

   ▸ Here is a famous excerpt from *The Feminine Mystique*: "The problem lay buried, unspoken, for many years in the minds of American women. It was a strange stirring, a sense of dissatisfaction, a yearning that women suffered in the middle of the twentieth century in the United States. Each suburban wife struggled with it alone. As she made the beds, shopped for groceries, matched slipcover material, ate peanut butter sandwiches with her children, chauffeured Cub Scouts and Brownies, lay beside her husband at night—she was afraid to ask even of herself the silent question—'Is this all?' "

   ▸ It is important to note that the above passage from *The Feminine Mystique* reflects the fact that, during the 1960s, feminism tended to be a movement of middle-class women.

Test Tip

Be sure that you can identify Betty Friedan. She was a leader in the women's rights movement.

2. The Expansion of Women's Rights

   ▸ All of the following contributed to the expansion of women's rights since 1963:

     — Title VII of the Civil Rights Act of 1964

     — Title IX (1972)

     — The Equal Credit Opportunity Act of 1974

— The Supreme Court decision in Roe v. Wade, allowing abortion

— Affirmative action regulations

X. COLD WAR CONFRONTATIONS: LATIN AMERICA

A. LATIN AMERICA

1. The Alliance for Progress

    ▶ The Alliance for Progress was initiated by President Kennedy in 1961. It aimed to establish economic cooperation between North America and South America.

    ▶ The Alliance for Progress was intended to counter the emerging Communist threat from Cuba.

2. The Bay of Pigs

    ▶ President Kennedy inherited from the Eisenhower administration a CIA-backed scheme to topple Fidel Castro from power by invading Cuba with anti-Communist exiles.

    ▶ When the invasion failed in 1961, Kennedy refused to rescue the insurgents, forcing them to surrender.

    ▶ Widely denounced as a fiasco, the Bay of Pigs defeat damaged U.S. credibility and characterized JFK as inexperienced and weak.

    ▶ The Bay of Pigs failure, along with continuing American covert efforts to assassinate Castro, pushed the Cuban dictator into a closer alliance with the Soviet Union.

    ▶ Soviet Premier Khrushchev responded by secretly sending nuclear missiles to Cuba.

3. The Cuban Missile Crisis (October 1962)

    ▶ The Cuban Missile Crisis was precipitated by the discovery of Soviet missile sites in Cuba.

▶ After a tense two weeks, the Soviets withdrew their missiles from Cuba in exchange for a promise from the United States not to attack Fidel Castro.

▶ As part of the negotiations to end the Cuban Missile Crisis, President Kennedy promised to refrain from a military invasion of Cuba.

XI. COLD WAR CONFRONTATIONS: THE VIETNAM WAR

A. THE TONKIN GULF RESOLUTION, 1964

1. An Incident in the Gulf of Tonkin

   ▶ The United States alleged that North Vietnamese torpedo boats launched an unprovoked attack against U.S. destroyers in the Gulf of Tonkin.

   ▶ The facts of what actually happened have never been fully explained.

2. The Resolution

   ▶ Congress responded to the unsubstantiated report of North Vietnamese aggression by overwhelmingly passing the Tonkin Gulf Resolution.

   ▶ The resolution authorized President Lyndon Johnson to "take all necessary measures to repel any armed attack against the forces of the United States and to prevent further aggression."

   ▶ The Tonkin Gulf Resolution gave President Johnson a blank check to escalate an undeclared war in Vietnam.

   ▶ Within a short time, President Johnson began to escalate the number of U.S. troops in Vietnam dramatically.

B. THE TET OFFENSIVE, 1968

1. What Happened?

   ▸ In late January 1968, the Viet Cong suddenly launched a series of attacks on twenty-seven key South Vietnamese cities, including the capital, Saigon.

   ▸ The Viet Cong were eventually forced to retreat after suffering heavy losses.

2. Consequences

   ▸ The Tet Offensive undermined President Johnson's credibility.

   ▸ As a result of the Tet Offensive, public support for the war decreased and antiwar sentiment increased.

   ▸ Partly as a result of the Tet Offensive, Johnson decided not to run for another term as president.

   ▸ The United States victory by the end of the Tet Offensive proved to be a classic "Pyrrhic victory" in that it won the battle but lost the war.

 XII. ## THE ANTIWAR MOVEMENT AND THE COUNTERCULTURE

A. PROTESTING GROUPS

1. During the 1960s, the following groups protested various aspects of American society:

   ▸ African Americans

   ▸ American Indians

   ▸ Women

   ▸ Youth (The Woodstock music festival was a counterculture gathering.)

   ▸ Hispanic Americans

B. ISSUES

1. The Vietnam War

2. Exclusion of women from the mainstream of U.S. life

3. Increasing bureaucratization and impersonal nature of U.S. life

4. Marginal economic status of minorities

5. The materialism of the United States

XIII. THE ELECTION OF 1968

A. DISSENSION WITHIN THE DEMOCRATIC PARTY

1. The assassination of Robert F. Kennedy (JFK's brother) left the Democratic Party divided between supporters of Vice President Hubert Humphrey and Senator Eugene McCarthy.

2. Humphrey won the nomination, but antiwar demonstrations at the Democratic National Convention in Chicago forced Humphrey to lead a badly divided party into the fall election.

B. GEORGE WALLACE AND WHITE BACKLASH

1. George Wallace, the former governor of Alabama, was a long-time champion of school segregation and states' rights.

2. Running as the candidate of the American Independent Party, Wallace's campaign appealed to Americans who were upset by the violence and civil disobedience associated with antiwar and civil rights demonstrations.

3. Wallace won five states in the South and received strong support in some Northern states.

C. THE RISE OF NIXON

1. The turmoil within the Democratic Party benefited former vice president Richard Nixon.

2. Nixon campaigned and won on a promise to restore law and order. He successfully appealed to many middle-class Americans fed up with years of riots and protests.

> *The 1968 presidential election was a pivotal political event of the 1960s. It revealed the cracks in U.S. society and was particularly disillusioning to young Americans. The decade of the 1960s had begun with hope and a favorable view of government. By the end of the decade, that optimism was gone for many young people.*

XIV. NIXON AND VIETNAM

A. THE DOVES DEMAND PEACE

1. Doves opposed the Vietnam War and staged massive demonstrations, demanding immediate troop withdrawals.

2. Senator William Fulbright was a leading dove. He wrote a critique of the war entitled *The Arrogance of Power*.

B. HAWKS AND THE SILENT MAJORITY SUPPORT NIXON

1. Hawks supported the Vietnam War, believing that withdrawing troops would be tantamount to surrender.

2. The Silent Majority was the name given by President Nixon to the moderate, mainstream Americans who quietly supported his Vietnam War policies. Members of the Silent Majority believed that the United States was justified in supporting South Vietnam.

C. THE INVASION OF CAMBODIA, 1970

1. Given the support of the Silent Majority, Nixon began to slowly withdraw U.S. troops from Vietnam and replace them with newly trained South Vietnamese troops.

2. The process of withdrawal and the training of Vietnamese troops was known as Vietnamization; the policy promised to preserve U.S. goals and bring "peace with honor."

3. The United States bombed and invaded Cambodia. On April 29, 1970, President Nixon, suddenly and without consulting Congress, ordered U.S. forces to join with the South Vietnamese army and clean out the Viet Cong sanctuaries in officially neutral Cambodia.

4. Nixon defended the action, saying that it was necessary to protect U.S. forces and support Vietnamization.

D. KENT STATE, 1970

1. Stunned by the invasion, college students across the nation erupted in protest.

2. More than 1.5 million angry students shut down 1,200 campuses.

3. At Kent State University in Ohio, a massive student protest led to the burning of the Reserve Officers' Training Corps (ROTC) building. In response to the growing unrest, the local mayor called in the National Guard.

4. Nervous members of the National Guard fired into a crowd of protesters, killing four students and wounding nine.

5. The Kent State shootings triggered massive antiwar rallies across the United States.

E. ENDING THE VIETNAM WAR

1. Henry Kissinger, President Nixon's national security adviser and top negotiator in Vietnam, engaged in a series of secret negotiations with the North Vietnamese, aimed at reaching a negotiated settlement.

2. The United States and the North Vietnamese finally reached an armistice: the Paris Accords, January 1973.

3. The United States agreed to withdraw the last of its troops. In exchange, the North Vietnamese released over 500 prisoners of war.

F. CONSEQUENCES OF THE VIETNAM WAR

1. The war affected the economy as follows:

▸ The United States could not afford both President Johnson's Great Society programs and the Vietnam War.

▸ The combination of spending on the war and expensive social programs produced the high inflation rates of the late 1960s and 1970s.

2. The war affected international involvements as follows:

▸ The Vietnam War increased public skepticism toward international involvements.

▸ In 1973, Congress passed the War Powers Act, which stipulated that the president must inform Congress within forty-eight hours if U.S. forces are sent into a hostile area without a declaration of war.

 XV. NIXON AND DÉTENTE

A. BACKGROUND OF DÉTENTE

1. The United States and the Communist world had been locked in a Cold War since the end of World War II.

2. The United States and the Soviet Union had experienced a series of tense Cold War confrontations that included the Berlin Airlift, the construction of the Berlin Wall, and the Cuban missile crisis.

3. Meanwhile, the United States had not formally recognized the Chinese Communist government.

4. Nixon and Henry Kissinger believed that the United States needed a new and more flexible foreign policy.

5. Détente called for a relaxation of tensions between the United States and the Communist world.

B. DÉTENTE AND CHINA

1. In late 1971, Nixon stunned the nation and the world by announcing that he intended to visit China, "to normalize relations between the two countries."

2. Nixon visited Beijing in February 1972. His trip to China marked a dramatic example of détente.

C. DÉTENTE AND THE SOVIET UNION

1. Just three months after becoming the first U.S. president to visit China, Nixon became the first U.S. president to visit Moscow.

2. Nixon's visit led to a series of agreements that reduced tensions between the United States and the Soviet Union. The most important agreements were:

   ▸ The Strategic Arms Limitation Talks (SALT). These talks led to the SALT I Treaty, which limited the number of intercontinental ballistic missiles and submarine-launched missiles each superpower could have in its arsenal.

   ▸ A series of agreements that expanded trade between the two superpowers.

XVI. NIXON AND THE NEW FEDERALISM

A. BACKGROUND

1. The Great Society programs had led to a dramatic increase in federal influence and federal spending.

2. Nixon wanted to reduce the size and influence of the federal government.

B. THE NEW FEDERALISM

1. Known as the New Federalism, Nixon's plan called for distributing a portion of federal power to state and local governments.

2. Under a program called revenue-sharing, state and local governments could spend their federal dollars however they saw fit, within certain limitations.

XVII. WATERGATE AND NIXON'S RESIGNATION

A. THE WATERGATE SCANDAL

1. A group of men hired by President Nixon's reelection committee were caught planting wiretaps in the Democratic National Committee offices at the Watergate office complex.

2. This began a series of steps by many Nixon assistants to cover up the involvement of the Nixon White House.

3. A Senate committee and a special prosecutor began investigations of illegal activities.

4. Nixon fired several of his top aides in an attempt to control the growing scandal.

B. NIXON'S RESIGNATION

1. As the House Judiciary Committee prepared to impeach Nixon for a series of crimes, members of the Republican Party encouraged him to resign.

2. In August 1974, Nixon became the first president to resign from office and Vice President Gerald Ford became president.

XVIII. THE CARTER ADMINISTRATION

A. JIMMY CARTER DEFEATED GERALD FORD IN 1976

1. Georgia governor Carter ran as an outsider against Ford.

2. Carter defeated Ford, who was a colorless campaigner.

B. THE ECONOMY

1. Inflation was the primary domestic issue during the Carter administration.

2. During the 1970s, the U.S. economy experienced both an increasing rate of inflation and a slowing of economic growth.

3. This somewhat unique combination of rising inflation and rising unemployment was called stagflation.

4. All of the following economic indicators increased during the Carter administration:

   ▶ Unemployment

   ▶ Inflation

   ▶ Government spending

   ▶ Gasoline prices (due to the 1973 Arab oil embargo and the 1979 revolution in Iran)

   ▶ Interest rates

5. All of the following were causes of inflationary pressure during the 1970s:

   ▶ Spending from the Vietnam War

   ▶ Rising energy costs

   ▶ Soaring federal budget deficits

   ▶ Rising healthcare costs

C. FOREIGN POLICY

1. President Carter emphasized a foreign policy based on human rights.

2. Carter's human rights policy aroused global concern and helped make human rights an international issue.

3. Carter was responsible for the Camp David Accords.

   ▶ In the summer of 1978, Carter invited the leaders of Egypt and Israel to Camp David—the presidential retreat in Maryland.

   ▶ After twelve days of intense negotiations, the leaders reached a peace agreement known as the Camp David Accords.

D. *BAKKE* DECISION

1. Affirmative action programs sought to provide more access to education and jobs for underrepresented minorities and women.

2. In the *Bakke* decision (1978), the Supreme Court ruled that quota systems were forbidden, but that affirmative action programs were constitutional.

E. THE 1980 ELECTION

1. The Iran hostage crisis played a key role in President Carter's defeat in the 1980 election.

2. Other factors that hurt Carter included the following:

   ▸ Double-digit inflation

   ▸ The energy crisis

   ▸ A perception of an indecisive and inept administration

PERIOD 9
——1980–PRESENT

Key Concepts†

Concept 1: A new conservatism grew to prominence in U.S. culture and politics, defending traditional social values and rejecting liberal views about the role of government.

Concept 2: The end of the Cold War and new challenges to U.S. leadership in the world forced the nation to redefine its foreign policy and global role.

Concept 3: Moving into the twenty-first century, the nation continued to experience challenges stemming from social, economic, and demographic changes.

I. REAGAN AND THE NEW CONSERVATISM

A. THE RISE OF REAGAN

1. As Jimmy Carter had done, Ronald Reagan capitalized on his status as a Washington outsider. (Reagan had been governor of California; Carter had been governor of Georgia.)

2. Key issues in the 1980 election included the following:

   ▸ The Iranian hostage crisis

   ▸ The weak economy and high rate of inflation

   ▸ Hostility toward big government

   ▸ Calls for a more conservative Supreme Court

B. REAGANOMICS

1. President Reagan implemented a series of economic policies known as "Reaganomics," or supply-side economics.

2. The key goals of Reaganomics were:

    ▸ Reduce federal tax rates for businesses and wealthy Americans. The Reagan tax cuts (based on a tactic used by Treasury Secretary Andrew Mellon in the 1920s) led to large increases in the incomes of wealthy Americans)

    ▸ Reduce corporate tax rates and encourage private investment

    ▸ Promote economic growth by deregulating business

C. FOREIGN POLICY

1. Iran-Contra Affair

    ▸ The United States secretly armed the anti-communist Contras in Nicaragua.

    ▸ The funding for this project came from secret arms sales to Iran in exchange for their help in freeing U.S. hostages in Lebanon.

    ▸ While Reagan testified that he had no prior knowledge of the affair, the scandal stained his administration.

2. Reagan challenged Soviet leader Gorbachev to end the division of Berlin by proclaiming "Tear down this wall" on a visit to the Berlin Wall.

3. Reagan and Gorbachev held four summit meetings to discuss strategic arms limitation.

D. DEMOGRAPHIC CHANGES

1. The 1970s witnessed a significant migration of Americans from the Frostbelt (the Northeast) to the Sunbelt (the South). This migration has continued to the present.

2. The South and West have experienced the greatest population gains since 1970.

3. The last twenty-five years have witnessed a significant increase in immigration from Latin America and Asia. The Immigration and Nationality Act of 1965 set this process in motion.

4. An aging population will ultimately threaten the long-term solvency of the Social Security and Medicare/Medicaid systems.

II. GEORGE H. W. BUSH

A. FOREIGN POLICY

1. Panamanian dictator Manuel Noriega was captured by U.S. forces and sentenced to forty years in prison for drug trafficking.

2. The East German government stopped enforcing border restrictions in 1989, effectively marking the end of the Berlin Wall.

3. Iraqi troops invaded Kuwait in 1991, leading to a coalition of forces led by the United States in Operation Desert Storm. After four days, Bush announced that Kuwait was liberated and that offensive operations were over. After the toppling of the Soviet Union, this successful military operation arguably marked a high point for U.S. foreign policy in the post-Vietnam era.

III. THE CLINTON PRESIDENCY

A. FOREIGN POLICY

1. The United States approved the North American Free Trade Agreement (NAFTA) in 1994, creating a North American trade bloc, the largest free trade zone in the world.

2. In the battle of Mogadishu, two U.S. helicopters were shot down and eighteen soldiers killed in an attempt to capture a Somali warlord.

3. Ethnic tensions in the Balkans led to U.S. support of North Atlantic Treaty Organization (NATO) military actions against Yugoslavia.

B. DOMESTIC POLICY

1. Clinton attempted to end discrimination against gays in the military.

2. After fierce opposition, he authorized a "don't ask, don't tell" compromise, which allowed gays to serve as long as their sexuality was secret.

C. LEWINSKY SCANDAL AND IMPEACHMENT

1. Clinton's sexual affair with twenty-two-year-old intern Monica Lewinsky led to an investigation by a special prosecutor.

2. Clinton was impeached by the House of Representatives for perjury and obstruction of justice.

3. The Senate voted to acquit Clinton on both charges.

IV. THE GEORGE W. BUSH PRESIDENCY

A. 2000 PRESIDENTIAL ELECTION

1. Despite winning more than 500,000 more popular votes than George W. Bush, Al Gore was unable to obtain a majority of electoral votes.

2. Disputed votes in Florida led to a Supreme Court decision, *Gore v. Bush*, which prevented a recount of ballots and made Bush president.

B. THE 9/11 ATTACKS AND AFGHANISTAN WAR

1. A group of Al-Qaeda terrorists used planes to destroy the two World Trade Center buildings in New York City and damage the Pentagon in Washington, D.C., on September 11, 2001. Another plane that may have been heading for Washington, D.C., was brought down in a field near Shanksville, Pennsylvania, when the passengers overtook the hijackers.

2. Close to 3,000 Americans were killed in the worst foreign attack on U.S. soil.

3. Congress passed the USA PATRIOT Act to provide law enforcement officials with greater latitude in pursuing terrorists.

    ▶ Wiretaps to track terrorists could be obtained more easily.

    ▶ Record searches could be conducted by the Federal Bureau of Investigation (FBI) and other law enforcement agencies without court orders.

4. The United States invaded Afghanistan for its Taliban government's harboring of Al-Qaeda leader Osama bin Laden.

5. After years of pursuit, bin Laden was captured and killed in Abbottabad, Pakistan, in a secret Navy SEAL mission in May 2011.

C. INVASION OF IRAQ

1. Believing that Iraqi dictator Saddam Hussein possessed weapons of mass destruction and had ties to Al-Qaeda, the United States led a coalition of nations to invade Iraq in March 2003.

2. After three weeks, the Iraqi government and military collapsed, and Saddam Hussein was captured, tried, and executed.

3. The war became increasingly unpopular in the United States as a result of numerous suicide bombings and U.S. casualties.

D. THE GREAT RECESSION DEVASTATES THE U.S. ECONOMY

1. Between October 2007 and March 2009, the Dow Jones Industrial Average dropped by over 50 percent, and real estate prices collapsed by over 30 percent in many markets around the country. As in past severe recessions and depressions (dating as far back as the Panic of 1819), poorly regulated financial markets led to loose lending practices, which in turn led to a boom-and-bust cycle.

2. The Great Recession followed the so-called Great Moderation (1982–2007), a long period of general prosperity for many, during which the economy suffered only two fairly mild recessions. After both of those recessions, however, the economy rebounded into what many economists have called a jobless recovery, wherein stock and real estate prices recovered much more quickly than a rise in employment. The same trends occurred after the Great Recession, which officially ended in June 2009.

 V. THE OBAMA PRESIDENCY

A. ELECTION OF BARACK OBAMA

1. Democratic Senator Barack Obama defeated Republican Senator John McCain to become America's first African American president in the 2008 presidential election.

2. Obama promised to withdraw from Iraq and supported universal health coverage.

3. McCain supported the Iraq war.

B. FIRST OBAMA ADMINISTRATION

1. Revolutionary demonstrations swept the Arab world in 2010 and 2011 in what became known as the Arab Spring.

2. Tunisian dictator Muammar Gaddafi of Libya was overthrown and killed by Libyan rebel troops.

3. The Affordable Health Care Act, popularly known as Obamacare, was passed in 2010 despite significant

controversy and opposition. This act has remained a key point of controversy between Democrats and Republicans.

C. SECOND OBAMA ADMINISTRATION

1. The Afghanistan war continued to plague U.S. policy makers, and President Obama promised to reduce troop involvement by early 2014.

2. A new crisis developed in the Mideast in 2014 as the Islamic State in Iraq and Syria (ISIS) gained control over a large amount of territory in both nations and engaged in terrorist activities, including executing journalists and aid workers.

3. By late 2014, the three key macroeconomic variables—the gross domestic product (GDP) growth rate of roughly 2 percent (versus a target range of 3 percent to 4 percent), unemployment of roughly 6 percent (versus a target range of 4 percent to 5 percent), and inflation of 2 percent (versus a target range of 1 percent to 2 percent)—showed an economy mostly stuck in neutral. By 2014, the United States had also amassed a national debt of approximately $18 trillion, a figure that severely limits government intervention (via spending programs or tax cuts). It also calls into question the standard of living of future generations because this large amount of debt must eventually be paid back.

PART III:

KEY THEMES
and Facts

KEY EVENTS AND FIGURES IN AFRICAN AMERICAN HISTORY
1619–1865

I. **FROM SERVITUDE TO SLAVERY IN THE CHESAPEAKE REGION, 1619–1690**

A. INDENTURED SERVANTS

1. The headright system enabled Chesapeake tobacco farmers to obtain both land and labor by importing workers from England.

2. English indentured servants were the chief source of agricultural labor in Virginia and Maryland before 1675. They accounted for 75 percent of the 130,000 English immigrants to Virginia and Maryland during the seventeenth century.

B. BACON'S REBELLION, 1676

1. The rebellion exposed tensions between backcountry farmers and the Tidewater gentry.

2. The rebellion prompted the Tidewater gentry to reevaluate their commitment to the system of indentured servants.

Test Tip

Bacon's Rebellion has significance for several areas of U.S. history, including slavery, political revolts, and class resentments. Be sure you know the causes and results of the rebellion.

C. THE BEGINNING OF SLAVERY

1. The profitable cultivation of tobacco required inexpensive labor.

2. Slave labor in colonial Virginia and Maryland spread rapidly in the last quarter of the seventeenth century, as blacks displaced white indentured servants in the tobacco fields.

II. GROWTH OF PLANTATION ECONOMIES AND SLAVE SOCIETIES, 1690–1754

A. THE SLAVE TRADE

1. In the seventeenth and eighteenth centuries, the vast majority of Africans who survived the transatlantic passage ended up working on plantations in Brazil and the Caribbean.

2. Of the slaves who crossed the Atlantic, only a relatively small number were brought into British North America.

B. SLAVERY IN THE AMERICAN COLONIES

1. Slavery was legally established in all thirteen colonies by the early 1700s.

2. Although enslaved, Africans maintained cultural practices brought from Africa.

3. Tobacco was the most important cash crop grown in the Chesapeake colonies. Rice was the most important cash crop grown in South Carolina.

4. Factors responsible for the development of slavery in the Southern colonies included the following:

   ▸ The supply of indentured servants from England became insufficient by the late seventeenth century.

   ▸ The spread of tobacco cultivation westward created a demand for labor.

> ▸ Few seventeenth- and early eighteenth-century white colonists viewed human bondage as morally unacceptable.

> ▸ As its maritime power increased, England wanted to compete in the profitable slave trade begun by the Portuguese and the Dutch.

C. THE STONO REBELLION, 1739

1. The Stono Rebellion was one of the earliest known acts of rebellion against slavery in America.

2. It was organized and led by slaves living south of Charleston, South Carolina. The slaves tried unsuccessfully to flee to Spanish Florida, where they hoped to gain their freedom.

The Stono Rebellion and Nat Turner's slave revolt (1831) were two of the most significant slave rebellions. Both revolts have appeared on previous AP exams, although the Stono Rebellion is mentioned most frequently.

III. GROWTH OF SLAVERY AND FREE BLACK COMMUNITIES, 1776–1815

A. THE DECLARATION OF INDEPENDENCE

1. The Declaration of Independence did *not* call for the abolition of the slave trade.

B. THE NORTHWEST ORDINANCE OF 1787

1. The Northwest Ordinance of 1787 excluded slavery north of the Ohio River.

2. The ordinance was the first national document containing a prohibition of slavery.

C. THE CONSTITUTION

1. As written in 1787, the U.S. Constitution explicitly guaranteed the legality of slavery in every state.

2. The Three-Fifths Compromise was an agreement between the Southern and Northern states. Under the terms of this compromise, three-fifths of the population of slaves would be counted for enumeration purposes regarding both the distribution of taxes and the apportionment of the members of the U.S. House of Representatives.

3. The Fourteenth Amendment invalidated the Three-Fifths Compromise. The amendment specifically states, "Representatives shall be apportioned . . . counting the whole number of persons in each state."

D. THE HAITIAN SLAVE REBELLION

1. The Haitian slave rebellion of the 1790s prompted an increased fear of slave revolts in the South.

2. The rebellion was led by Toussaint L'Ouverture.

E. FREE AFRICAN AMERICANS

1. The following factors contributed to the growth of the free African American population:

   ▸ The gradual emancipation laws of individual states

   ▸ Manumission granted for Revolutionary War service

   ▸ Manumission granted by slaveholders' wills

   ▸ Natural increase among free African Americans

IV. PLANTERS AND SLAVES IN THE ANTEBELLUM SOUTH, 1816–1860

A. KING COTTON

1. The following factors contributed to making cotton the South's most important cash crop:

> ▸ The invention of the cotton gin made it possible and profitable to harvest short-staple cotton.

> ▸ Rich new farmland in the Deep South was opened to the cultivation of cotton. By 1850, the geographic center of slavery was moving southward and westward.

> ▸ The rise of textile manufacturing in England created enormous demand for cotton.

B. SOUTHERN SOCIETY

1. It is very important to remember that a majority of white adult males were small farmers rather than wealthy planters.

2. The majority of white families in the antebellum South owned no slaves.

3. Nonetheless, a small minority of planters who owned twenty or more slaves dominated the antebellum South.

4. The cost of slave labor rose sharply between 1800 and 1860.

C. SLAVE SOCIETY

1. Despite forced separations, slaves maintained social networks among kindred and friends.

2. The dramatic increase in the South's slave labor force was due to the natural population increase of American-born slaves.

3. During the antebellum period, free African Americans were able to accumulate some property in spite of discrimination.

4. Although Southern legal codes did not uniformly provide for the legalization and stability of slave marriage, slaves were generally able to marry, and the institution of marriage was common on Southern plantations.

5. The majority of slaves adapted to the oppressive conditions imposed on them by developing a separate African American culture.

KEY THEMES AND FACTS

6. Slave revolts were infrequent. Most Southern slaves resisted their masters by feigning illness and working as slowly as possible.

 V. **TERRITORIAL EXPANSION AND SLAVERY, 1820–1860**

A. THE MISSOURI COMPROMISE OF 1820

1. Provisions of the Missouri Compromise included the following:

   ▸ Maine would enter the Union as a free state.

   ▸ Missouri would enter the Union as a slave state.

   ▸ The remaining territory of the Louisiana Purchase above latitude 36°30′ would be closed to slavery.

2. Consequences of the Missouri Compromise included the following:

   ▸ The number of Northerners and Southerners in the Senate remained the same.

   ▸ Most of the Louisiana Purchase was closed to slavery.

   ▸ The first major nineteenth-century conflict over slavery was settled.

   ▸ Slavery was temporarily defused as a national political issue.

B. TEXAS

1. President Jackson resisted the admission of Texas into the Union in 1836, primarily because he feared that the debate over the admission of Texas would ignite controversy over slavery.

2. Following a joint resolution of Congress, Texas joined the Union in December 1845.

C. THE WILMOT PROVISO

1. The Wilmot Proviso specifically provided for the prohibition of slavery in lands acquired from Mexico in the Mexican War.

2. Congress did *not* pass the Wilmot Proviso.

D. THE COMPROMISE OF 1850

1. California was admitted to the Union as a free state.

2. Slave trade (but not slavery) was abolished in the District of Columbia.

3. Territorial governments were created in New Mexico and Utah without an immediate decision as to whether they would be slave or free.

4. A stringent measure—the enhanced Fugitive Slave Act—was enacted. The act proved to be the most controversial and divisive component of the Compromise of 1850.

E. OSTEND MANIFESTO, 1854

1. The manifesto was a proposal to seize Cuba by force.

2. Enraged antislavery Northerners prevented it from being implemented.

F. THE KANSAS-NEBRASKA ACT, 1854

1. Provisions of the act included the following:

    ▸ The proposed Territory of Nebraska would be divided into two territories, Kansas and Nebraska.

    ▸ The status of slavery would be settled by popular sovereignty.

    ▸ Popular sovereignty meant that the settlers in a given territory would have the sole right to decide whether or not slavery would be permitted.

▶ Senator Stephen A. Douglas was the leading proponent of popular sovereignty. Here is how Douglas explained the doctrine of popular sovereignty: "The great principle is the right of every community to judge and decide for itself whether a thing is right or wrong. . . . It is no answer to this argument to say that slavery is an evil, and hence should not be tolerated. You must allow the people to decide for themselves whether it is a good or an evil."

2. Consequences of the Kansas-Nebraska Act:

▶ It repealed the Missouri Compromise, thus heightening sectional tensions.

▶ It led to the demise of the Whigs.

▶ It led to the rise of the Republican Party and Abraham Lincoln.

▶ Kansas became the first test of popular sovereignty.

G. THE *DRED SCOTT* DECISION, 1857

1. The Supreme Court ruled that black people were not citizens of the United States and therefore could not petition the Court.

2. The *Dred Scott* decision established the principle that national legislation could not limit the spread of slavery into the territories.

3. By stating that Congress had no right to prohibit slavery in the territories, the *Dred Scott* decision repealed the Northwest Ordinance of 1787 and the Missouri Compromise of 1820.

4. The *Dred Scott* decision became a contentious issue during the Lincoln–Douglas debates. It also significantly increased regional tensions and thus was a key cause leading to the Civil War.

H. THE POSITIONS OF THE REPUBLICANS AND DEMOCRATS ON SLAVERY

1. The Democratic Party was divided on the issue of expanding slavery into the territories.

2. The Republican Party opposed the extension of slavery into the territories (as such, Republicans embraced the free soil position established by the Wilmot Proviso). However, the Republicans acknowledged that slavery should be protected in the states where it already existed.

VI. ABOLITION AND THE ABOLITIONISTS, 1830–1860

A. THE SECOND GREAT AWAKENING

1. The religious spirit of the Second Great Awakening increased public awareness of the moral outrages perpetuated by slavery.

2. It also contributed to the growth of the abolitionist movement.

B. AMERICAN COLONIZATION SOCIETY

1. The goal of the American Colonization Society was to return freed slaves to Africa.

2. The leaders of the American Colonization Society were middle-class men and women.

C. WILLIAM LLOYD GARRISON

1. Garrison issued the first call for the "immediate and uncompensated emancipation of the slaves."

2. Here is a famous quote from the first issue of *The Liberator*: "Let Southern oppressors tremble . . . I will be as harsh as Truth and as uncompromising as Justice . . . I am in earnest—I will not retreat a single inch—and I WILL BE HEARD!"

D. FREDERICK DOUGLASS

1. Frederick Douglass was the most prominent black abolitionist during the antebellum period.

2. Published in 1845, Douglass's autobiography, *Narrative of the Life of Frederick Douglass, an American Slave,* exposed Americans to the horrors and inhumanity of slavery.

3. Although best known as an abolitionist, Douglass also championed equal rights for women and Native Americans. He often declared, "I would unite with anybody to do right and with nobody to do wrong."

E. HARRIET BEECHER STOWE

1. Harriet Beecher Stowe wrote *Uncle Tom's Cabin.*

2. *Uncle Tom's Cabin* intensified Northern opposition to slavery. Only the Bible sold more copies.

VII. EMANCIPATION AND THE ROLE OF AFRICAN AMERICANS IN THE CIVIL WAR, 1861–1865

A. THE EMANCIPATION PROCLAMATION, 1863

1. President Lincoln refrained from taking action to emancipate slaves until the Civil War had been in progress for almost two years. Lincoln delayed because he wanted to retain the loyalty of the border states.

2. The Union victory at Antietam gave Lincoln the opportunity to issue the Emancipation Proclamation.

3. The Emancipation Proclamation only freed slaves in the rebellious states.

4. The Emancipation Proclamation did *not* free slaves in the border states.

5. The immediate effect of the Emancipation Proclamation was to strengthen the moral cause of the Union, which in turn helped keep Great Britain and France from supporting the South in the Civil War.

B. AFRICAN AMERICANS AT WAR

1. For most of the Civil War, African American soldiers were paid less than white soldiers of equal rank.

2. The South considered African Americans serving in the Union army as contraband.

KEY EVENTS AND FIGURES IN AFRICAN AMERICAN HISTORY
1865–Present

I. RECONSTRUCTION AND THE NEW SOUTH, 1865–1896

A. THE RECONSTRUCTION AMENDMENTS

1. The Thirteenth Amendment abolished slavery and involuntary servitude.

2. The Fourteenth Amendment had three key components:

   ▶ First, it made former slaves citizens, thus invalidating the *Dred Scott* decision.

   ▶ Second, it stated, "[N]or shall any State deprive any person of life, liberty, or property without due process of law; nor deny to any person within its jurisdiction the equal protection of the laws."

   ▶ Third, it protected recently passed congressional legislation guaranteeing civil rights to former slaves.

3. The Fifteenth Amendment provided suffrage for black males.

B. SHARECROPPERS

1. The majority of freedmen entered sharecropping arrangements with former masters and other nearby planters.

2. Sharecropping and the crop lien system led to a cycle of debt and depression for Southern tenant farmers.

3. A rumor circulating among the freed slaves suggested that they would each receive "forty acres and a mule." This redistribution of wealth never occurred.

C. BLACK CODES

1. Black Codes were intended to place limits on the socioeconomic opportunities and freedoms open to black people.

2. Black Codes forced black Americans to work under conditions that closely resembled slavery.

D. THE COMPROMISE OF 1877

1. The Compromise called for the removal of all federal troops from the South.

2. It supported internal improvements in the South.

3. It promised there would be at least one Southerner in the president's cabinet.

4. It gave conservative Southern Democrats some control over local patronage.

5. It gave the South a "free hand" in race relations. As a result, white conservatives returned to power, lynchings increased, and black voters were disenfranchised.

E. THE 1873 SLAUGHTERHOUSE CASES AND THE 1883 CIVIL RIGHTS CASES

1. Both cases narrowed the meaning and effectiveness of the Fourteenth Amendment.

2. Both cases weakened the protection given to African Americans under the Fourteenth Amendment.

F. *PLESSY v. FERGUSON*, 1896

1. The *Plessy v. Ferguson* decision upheld segregated railroad facilities.

2. The Supreme Court decision in *Plessy v. Ferguson* sanctioned "separate but equal" public facilities for African Americans.

G. DISENFRANCHISING BLACK VOTERS

1. Southern politicians used a number of tactics to disenfranchise black voters:

   ‣ Literacy tests and poll taxes were used to deny African Americans the ballot.

   ‣ The grandfather clause exempted freed slaves from literacy tests and poll taxes provided they had a grandfather who had voted in 1860. Unfortunately, slaves did not vote at that time.

   ‣ Electoral districts were gerrymandered to favor the Democratic Party.

H. BOOKER T. WASHINGTON

1. In his Atlanta Compromise speech (1895), Booker T. Washington called on blacks to seek economic opportunities rather than political rights. Here is an excerpt from his speech: "In all things purely social we can be as separate as the fingers, yet one as the hand in all things essential to mutual progress."

2. Booker T. Washington particularly stressed the importance of vocational education and economic self-help. Washington urged black Americans to avoid public political agitation.

3. Booker T. Washington supported all of the following:

   ‣ Accommodation to white society

   ‣ Economic self-help

   ‣ Industrial education

4. Washington opposed public political agitation.

II. BLACK AMERICANS DURING THE PROGRESSIVE ERA, 1897–1917

A. W.E.B. DU BOIS

1. During the Progressive Era, W.E.B. Du Bois emerged as the most influential advocate of full political, economic, and social equality for black Americans.

2. Du Bois founded the National Association for the Advancement of Colored People (NAACP) in 1909.

3. Du Bois advocated the intellectual development of a "talented tenth" of the black population. Du Bois hoped that this talented tenth would become influential through methods such as continuing their education, writing books, or becoming directly involved in social change.

4. Du Bois opposed the implementation of Booker T. Washington's program for gradual black progress.

It is important to understand the different approaches of Booker T. Washington and W.E.B. Du Bois. Remember, Washington stressed economic self-help before pushing for political and social equality, while Du Bois stressed fighting for full political and social rights.

B. THE NAACP

1. The NAACP rejected Booker T. Washington's gradualism and separatism.

2. The NAACP focused on using the courts to achieve equality and justice.

C. THE PROGRESSIVES

1. Civil rights laws for black Americans were not part of the Progressive program of reforms.

2. Progressive Era legislation showed little concern for ending racial segregation.

D. IDA B. WELLS-BARNETT

1. Ida B. Wells-Barnett was an African American civil rights advocate and an early women's rights advocate.

2. She was the principal public opponent of lynching in the South.

E. THE BIRTH OF A NATION AND THE KU KLUX KLAN

1. The Ku Klux Klan (KKK) first emerged during Radical Reconstruction (1865–1877).

2. D. W. Griffith's epic film *The Birth of a Nation* (1915) became controversial because of its depiction of KKK activities as heroic and commendable.

3. *The Birth of a Nation* played a role in the resurgence of the KKK during the Progressive Era.

4. The KKK favored white supremacy and immigration restriction.

F. WORLD WAR I

1. African Americans fought in strictly segregated units, usually under the command of white officers.

2. The first massive migration of black Americans from the South occurred during and immediately after World War I.

 ## III. THE 1920S

A. THE HARLEM RENAISSANCE

1. The Harlem Renaissance thrived during the 1920s.

2. It was an outpouring of black artistic and literary creativity.

3. Harlem Renaissance writers and artists expressed pride in their African American culture.

4. Key figures in the Harlem Renaissance included James Weldon Johnson, Langston Hughes, Zora Neale Hurston, and Josephine Baker.

B. MARCUS GARVEY

1. Marcus Garvey was the leader of the Universal Negro Improvement Association.

2. Garveyism was identified with the following:

   ▸ Black pride

   ▸ Black economic development

   ▸ Black nationalism

   ▸ Pan-Africanism

3. Garvey was committed to the idea that black Americans should return to Africa.

Frederick Douglass, Booker T. Washington, W.E.B. Du Bois, and Dr. Martin Luther King, Jr., are America's best-known civil rights leaders. You should study these leaders, but do not neglect Ida B. Wells-Barnett and Marcus Garvey.

IV. THE GREAT DEPRESSION AND THE NEW DEAL, 1929–1941

A. THE NEW DEAL

1. New Deal programs did help African Americans survive the Great Depression.

2. The New Deal did *not* directly confront racial segregation and injustice. As a result, there was no major action on civil rights.

B. SHIFT IN VOTING PATTERNS

1. As a result of the Emancipation Proclamation and the Reconstruction amendments, African Americans were loyal voters for the Republican Party.

2. The presidency of Franklin D. Roosevelt witnessed a major shift of black voters from the Republican Party to the Democratic Party.

C. ELEANOR ROOSEVELT AND THE DAUGHTERS OF THE AMERICAN REVOLUTION

1. In 1939, the Daughters of the American Revolution (DAR) barred Marian Anderson, a world-renowned African American singer, from performing at Constitution Hall in Washington, D.C.

2. Outraged by this action, Eleanor Roosevelt resigned from the DAR.

3. Roosevelt's dramatic act of conscience gave national attention to the issue of racial discrimination.

V. WORLD WAR II, 1941–1945

A. THE HOME FRONT

1. The black migration from the South to the North and West continued.

2. Under pressure from A. Philip Randolph, a prominent African American leader, President Roosevelt issued an executive order forbidding discrimination in defense industries. The order was monitored by the Fair Employment Practices Commission.

B. THE WAR

1. Black Americans continued to fight in segregated units. The armed forces were not racially integrated during World War II.

KEY THEMES AND FACTS

THE MODERN CIVIL RIGHTS MOVEMENT, 1945 – PRESENT

A. PRESIDENT HARRY S. TRUMAN

1. President Truman issued an executive order to desegregate the armed forces in 1948.

2. The Dixiecrats walked out of the 1948 Democratic National Convention to demonstrate their opposition to President Truman's civil rights legislation.

B. *BROWN v. BOARD OF EDUCATION OF TOPEKA*, 1954

1. The Supreme Court ruled that segregation in public schools was a denial of the equal protection of the laws guaranteed in the Fourteenth Amendment.

2. The Supreme Court decision directly contradicted the legal principle of "separate but equal" established by *Plessy v. Ferguson* in 1896.

3. As a result of its victory in *Brown v. Board of Education of Topeka,* the NAACP continued to base its court suits on the Equal Protection Clause of the Fourteenth Amendment.

C. PRESIDENT EISENHOWER

1. President Dwight D. Eisenhower sent federal troops to Little Rock's Central High School to enforce court-ordered desegregation.

2. Eisenhower supported his decision by saying, "The very basis of our individual rights and freedoms rests upon the certainty that the President and the Executive Branch of Government will support and insure the carrying out of the decisions of the federal courts, even, when necessary, with all the means at the President's command."

3. Although President Eisenhower did send troops to Little Rock, he was not a vigorous supporter of civil rights legislation.

4. The primary power granted to the Civil Rights Commission in 1957 was the authority to investigate and report on cases involving discrimination.

D. DR. MARTIN LUTHER KING, JR.

1. Dr. King's goal was a peaceful integration of the races into all areas of society.

2. His theory of nonviolent civil disobedience was influenced by the writings of Henry David Thoreau.

3. Dr. King was head of the Southern Christian Leadership Conference (SCLC).

4. In his "Letter from Birmingham Jail," Dr. King argued that citizens have "a moral responsibility to disobey unjust laws." Dr. King believed that civil disobedience is justified in the face of unjust laws.

5. The following quotation vividly expresses Dr. King's nonviolent philosophy:

> *"The problem with hatred and violence is that they intensify the fears of the White majority, and leave them less ashamed of their prejudices toward Negroes. In the guilt and confusion confronting our society, violence only adds to chaos. It deepens the brutality of the oppressor and increases the bitterness of the oppressed. Violence is the antithesis of creativity and wholeness. It destroys community and makes brotherhood impossible."*

E. THE SIT-IN MOVEMENT

1. College students staged the first sit-ins in Greensboro, North Carolina, in 1960 to protest segregation in public facilities.

2. The sit-ins provide an excellent example of nonviolent civil disobedience.

F. MALCOLM X

1. Malcolm X and Stokely Carmichael opposed Dr. King's strategy of nonviolent demonstration.

2. Malcolm X was a key leader of the Black Muslims.

KEY THEMES AND FACTS

G. KEY CIVIL RIGHTS LEADERS

1. Dr. King—Southern Christian Leadership Conference (SCLC)

2. Roy Wilkins—NAACP

3. Stokely Carmichael—Student Nonviolent Coordinating Committee (SNCC)

4. Huey Newton—Black Panthers

5. Malcolm X—Black Muslims

H. BLACK LEADERS WHO FAVORED SEPARATISM

1. Marcus Garvey—back-to-Africa movement

2. Elijah Muhammad—the Black Muslim movement

3. Stokely Carmichael—the Black Power movement

4. Huey Newton—the Black Panther movement

I. BLACK POWER

1. The Black Power movement of the late 1960s advocated that African Americans establish control of their economic and political lives.

2. Huey Newton (Black Panthers) and Stokely Carmichael (SNCC) were spokespeople for black Power.

3. The Black Panthers and the Nation of Islam emphasized a greater sense of Black nationalism and solidarity.

J. ELECTION OF BARACK OBAMA, 2008

1. In November 2008, a record number of voters elected Barack Obama as the nation's forty-forth president.

2. Obama thus became America's first African American president.

3. Obama's winning coalition included minorities, college-educated whites, and young voters aged 18 to 26.

KEY EVENTS AND FIGURES IN WOMEN'S HISTORY

I. LIFE IN COLONIAL AMERICA, 1607–1789

A. ANNE HUTCHINSON

1. Anne Hutchinson challenged Puritan religious authorities, including founder John Winthrop, in Massachusetts Bay.

2. Puritan authorities banished Anne Hutchinson because she challenged religious doctrine, gender roles, and clerical authority, and she claimed to have had revelations from God.

B. LEGAL STATUS OF COLONIAL WOMEN

1. Women usually lost control of their property when they married.

2. Married women had no separate legal identity apart from their husbands.

3. Women could *not* hold political office, serve as clergy, vote, or serve as jurors.

4. Single women and widows did have the legal right to own property.

5. Women serving as indentured servants had to remain unmarried until the period of their indenture was over.

C. THE CHESAPEAKE COLONIES

1. There was a scarcity of women and a high mortality rate among men. This was especially true in the seventeenth century.

2. As a result of the scarcity of women, the status of women in the Chesapeake colonies was higher than that of women in the New England colonies.

II. THE EARLY REPUBLIC, 1789–1815

A. ABIGAIL ADAMS

1. Abigail Adams was an early proponent of women's rights.

2. Here is an excerpt from the famous letter she wrote to her husband, John Adams:

   ". . . [A]nd by the way in the new code of laws which I suppose it will be necessary for you to make, I desire you would remember the ladies, and be more generous and favorable to them than your ancestors. . . . Remember, men would be tyrants if they could."

3. Abigail Adams's letter demonstrates that some colonial women hoped to benefit from republican ideals of equality and individual rights.

Sadly, John Adams ignored his wife's plea to "remember the ladies." Although ignored by the framers of the Constitution, Abigail's letter has been frequently remembered by APUSH test writers. You should be able to identify the quotation and know the basics of republican motherhood.

B. THE CULT OF DOMESTICITY/REPUBLICAN MOTHERHOOD

1. The term *cult of domesticity* refers to the idealization of women in their roles as wives and mothers.

2. The term *republican motherhood* suggested that women would be responsible for rearing their children to become virtuous citizens of the new American republic. By emphasizing family and religious values, women could have a positive moral influence on the American political character.

3. Middle-class Americans viewed the home as a refuge from the world rather than a productive economic unit.

4. Catharine Beecher supported the cult of domesticity. Here is an illustrative quotation:

> *"The mother writes the character of the future man; the sister bends the fibers that hereafter are the forest tree; the wife sways the heart, whose energies may turn for good or evil the destinies of a nation. Let the women of a country be virtuous and intelligent, and the men will certainly be the same."*

III. WOMEN IN ANTEBELLUM AMERICA, 1815–1860

A. THE LOWELL SYSTEM

1. The Lowell System was a plan developed in the early nineteenth century to promote and expand textile manufacturing.

2. During the first half of the nineteenth century, textile mills in Lowell, Massachusetts, relied heavily on a labor force of women and children.

3. During the 1820s and 1830s, the majority of workers in the textile mills of Massachusetts were young unmarried women from rural New England who sought to earn money of their own.

4. Prior to the Civil War, Irish immigrants began to replace New England farm girls in the textile mills.

B. THE SENECA FALLS CONVENTION, 1848

1. The Seneca Falls Convention was organized and led by Elizabeth Cady Stanton and Lucretia Mott.

2. The Seneca Falls Convention called for women's rights in the following areas:

   ▸ Suffrage

   ▸ The right to retain property after marriage

KEY THEMES AND FACTS

   ▶ Equal educational opportunities

   ▶ Divorce and child custody rights

3. The "Declaration of Sentiments and Resolutions" issued by the Seneca Falls Convention demanded greater rights for women. The declaration's first sentence clearly states this goal: "We hold these truths to be self-evident: that all men and women are created equal."

C. CHARACTERISTICS OF THE WOMEN'S MOVEMENT IN THE ANTEBELLUM PERIOD

1. The movement was led by middle-class women.

2. It promoted a broad-based platform of legal and educational rights.

3. It had close links with the antislavery and temperance movements.

4. It held conventions in the Northeast and Midwest but not in the South.

5. It supported all of the following goals:

   ▶ Right of women to vote

   ▶ Abolition of slavery

   ▶ Passage of temperance laws

   ▶ Right of married women to own property

D. SARAH MOORE GRIMKÉ

1. She was one of the first women to support abolition and women's suffrage publicly.

2. Here is a famous quotation by Grimké, advocating women's rights:

   "I ask no favors for my sex. I surrender not our claim to equality. All I ask of our brethren is that they will take their feet off our necks."

REFORMERS AND SUFFRAGETTES, 1865–1920

A. JANE ADDAMS

1. Jane Addams is best known for founding Hull House in Chicago. (Note: Jane Addams was not an abolitionist.)

2. Hull House and other settlement houses became centers of women's activism and reform efforts to help the urban poor. Settlement house workers engaged in all of the following:

   ▸ Teaching classes on cooking and dressmaking

   ▸ Publishing reports on deplorable housing conditions

   ▸ Offering literacy and language classes for immigrants

   ▸ Establishing day nurseries for working mothers

B. THE FIGHT FOR SUFFRAGE

1. Frontier life tended to promote the acceptance of greater equality for women.

2. The only states with complete women's suffrage before 1900 were located west of the Mississippi. Wyoming (1869) was the first state to grant women the full right to vote.

3. The Nineteenth Amendment (1920) guaranteed women the right to vote.

C. THE WOMEN'S CHRISTIAN TEMPERANCE UNION

1. Carry Nation was one of the best known and most outspoken leaders of the Women's Christian Temperance Union (WCTU).

2. The WCTU successfully convinced many women that they had a moral responsibility to improve society by working for prohibition.

D. WOMEN AND THE PROGRESSIVE REFORMS

1. Dorothea Dix worked tirelessly on behalf of the mentally ill.

KEY THEMES AND FACTS

2. Ida B. Wells-Barnett was an African American civil rights advocate and an early women's rights advocate. She is noted for her opposition to lynching.

3. Women reformers were also actively involved in the following Progressive Era reforms:

   ▸ Passage of child-labor legislation at the state level

   ▸ Campaigns to limit the working hours of women and children

E. WOMEN AND THE WORKPLACE

1. During the late nineteenth and early twentieth centuries, the majority of female workers employed outside the home were young and unmarried.

2. During the late nineteenth and early twentieth centuries, women were most likely to work outside their homes as one of the following:

   ▸ Domestic servants

   ▸ Garment workers

   ▸ Teachers

   ▸ Cigar makers

3. During the late nineteenth century, women were least likely to work outside their homes as any of the following:

   ▸ Physicians

   ▸ Lawyers

BOOM AND BUST, 1920–1940

A. FLAPPERS

1. Flappers symbolized the new freedom by challenging traditional U.S. attitudes about women. They favored short bobbed hair, smoked cigarettes, and even wore the new one-piece bathing suits.

2. In reality, few women actually lived the flapper lifestyle. Nonetheless, the look was very fashionable among college coeds, office workers, and store clerks.

B. WOMEN AND THE WORKFORCE

1. Although new jobs became available in offices and stores, the percentage of single women in the labor force actually declined between 1920 and 1930.

2. Women did not receive equal pay and continued to face discrimination in the professions.

3. Most married women did not seek employment outside the home.

C. MARGARET SANGER

1. Margaret Sanger was an outspoken reformer who openly championed birth control for women.

D. DECLINE OF THE FEMINIST MOVEMENT

1. The following factors caused a decline in the organized feminist movement during the 1920s:

   ▸ The passage of the Nineteenth Amendment granting women the right to vote

   ▸ Changing manners and morality symbolized by the flappers

   ▸ Dissension among women's groups concerning goals

   ▸ The decline of the Progressive Era reform movement

E. ELEANOR ROOSEVELT

1. Eleanor Roosevelt was a strong supporter of women's rights during the period of the New Deal.

VI. WOMEN AND THE WORKPLACE, 1941–1960

A. WORLD WAR II

1. World War II stimulated a widespread movement of women into factory work.

2. During World War II, married women entered the workforce in large numbers.

3. Rosie the Riveter was a nickname given to women who worked in America's factories during World War II.

B. THE 1950S

1. Following World War II, women were encouraged to give up their factory jobs and return home, where they would devote themselves to being wives and mothers.

 VII. THE MODERN WOMEN'S RIGHTS MOVEMENT

A. BETTY FRIEDAN

1. Betty Friedan wrote *The Feminine Mystique* and was a founder and the first president of the National Organization for Women (NOW).

2. NOW was founded in 1966 to challenge sex discrimination in the workplace.

3. Here is a famous excerpt from her book *The Feminine Mystique*:

> "The problem lay buried, unspoken, for many years in the minds of American women. It was a strange stirring, a sense of dissatisfaction, a yearning that women suffered in the middle of the twentieth century in the United States. Each suburban wife struggled with it alone. As she made the beds, shopped for groceries, matched slipcover material, ate peanut butter sandwiches with her children, chauffeured Cub Scouts and Brownies, lay beside her husband at night—she was afraid to ask even of herself the silent question—'Is this all?' "

4. It is important to note that the passage from Friedan reflects the fact that feminism tended to be a movement of middle-class women.

5. Betty Friedan is best known for her criticism of traditional gender roles.

B. THE EXPANSION OF WOMEN'S RIGHTS SINCE 1963

1. All of the following contributed to the expansion of women's rights since 1963:

   ▶ Title VII of the Civil Rights Act of 1964

   ▶ Title IX of the Education Amendments of 1972

   ▶ The Equal Credit Opportunity Act of 1974

   ▶ The Supreme Court decision in *Roe v. Wade*

   ▶ Affirmative action regulations

C. THE EQUAL RIGHTS AMENDMENT

1. The Equal Rights Amendment (ERA) did not pass. So the ERA is not an amendment.

2. Phyllis Schlafly led a campaign to block ratification of the Equal Rights Amendment.

D. FEMALE VICE PRESIDENTIAL CANDIDATES

1. Geraldine Ferraro was the first woman nominated for vice president by a major political party. She was Democrat Walter Mondale's running mate in 1984.

2. Sarah Palin was the first woman nominated for vice president by the Republican Party. She was John McCain's running mate in 2008.

KEY THEMES AND FACTS

KEY EVENTS IN NATIVE AMERICAN HISTORY

I. PRECONTACT SOCIETIES

A. ARRIVAL IN NORTH AMERICA

1. Most scholars now believe that the first Native Americans reached North America by traveling across a land bridge connecting eastern Siberia and Alaska.

B. KEY ADVANCES

1. Precontact peoples developed all of the following:

   ▸ A mathematically based calendar

   ▸ Irrigation systems

   ▸ Domesticated cereal crops such as maize

   ▸ Multifamily dwellings

   ▸ Herbal medical treatments

   ▸ Large cities such as the Aztec capital of Tenochtitlán

C. KEY FAILURES

1. Precontact peoples did *not* develop the following:

   ▸ Wheeled vehicles

   ▸ Gunpowder

   ▸ Waterwheels

Many AP U.S. History courses pay little attention to precontact history, and APUSH exams rarely contain questions on this time period. Plan your study time accordingly.

II. FIRST EUROPEAN CONTACTS WITH NATIVE AMERICANS

A. COLUMBIAN EXCHANGE

1. The term *Columbian Exchange* refers to the exchange of plants and animals between the New World and Europe following the discovery of America in 1492.

2. New World crops such as corn, tomatoes, and potatoes had a dramatic effect on the European diet. At the same time, Old World domesticated animals such as horses, cows, and pigs had a dramatic effect on life in the New World.

B. DISEASE AND POPULATION COLLAPSE

1. Old World diseases caused epidemics among Native American inhabitants of the New World.

2. Native Americans suffered severe population declines because they lacked immunity to smallpox and other European diseases.

C. SIMILARITIES BETWEEN NATIVE AMERICANS AND THE FIRST ENGLISH SETTLERS

1. Both had agricultural economies.

2. Both lived in village communities.

3. Both domesticated corn and other vegetables.

4. Both shared a strong sense of spirituality.

D. DIFFERENCES BETWEEN NATIVE AMERICANS AND THE FIRST ENGLISH SETTLERS

1. Native Americans and English settlers had radically different conceptions of property.

2. The English had a very precise concept of private property rights.

3. Native Americans had no concept of private property.

4. These first English settlers tended to be Christians, and many considered the Native Americans to be heathens who should be converted.

E. INTERACTION BETWEEN NATIVE AMERICANS AND ENGLISH SETTLERS

1. The more Native Americans interacted with the English colonists, the more dependent the Native Americans became on the fur trade.

2. Political and linguistic differences among Native Americans hindered united opposition to the English.

F. THE IROQUOIS CONFEDERACY

1. The Iroquois Confederacy was the most important and powerful Native American alliance.

2. The tribes of the Iroquois Confederacy formed the most important Native American political organization to confront the colonists.

3. During the eighteenth century, the Iroquois lived in permanent settlements.

Test Tip

APUSH test writers do not expect you to know the names of specific Native American tribes. However, be sure that you can identify the Iroquois Confederacy.

III. FORCED REMOVAL OF AMERICAN INDIANS TO THE TRANS-MISSISSIPPI WEST

A. *WORCESTER v. GEORGIA* (1831)

1. The Cherokee differed from other Native American tribes in that the Cherokee tried to mount a court challenge to a removal order.

2. In the case of *Worcester v. Georgia,* the U.S. Supreme Court upheld the rights of the Cherokee tribe to their tribal lands.

B. ANDREW JACKSON AND THE CHEROKEES

1. President Jackson refused to recognize the Court's decision; he said, "John Marshall has made his decision: now let him enforce it."

2. Jackson's antipathy toward Native Americans was well known: "I have long viewed treaties with American Indians as an absurdity not to be reconciled to the principles of our government."

C. THE TRAIL OF TEARS

1. Jackson's Native American policy resulted in the removal of the Cherokee from their homeland to settlements across the Mississippi River.

2. The Trail of Tears refers to the relocation of Native Americans to settlements in what is now Oklahoma.

3. Approximately one-quarter of the Cherokee people died on the Trail of Tears.

 IV. GOVERNMENT POLICY TOWARD AMERICAN INDIANS IN THE SECOND HALF OF THE NINETEENTH CENTURY

A. DECLINE OF THE PLAINS INDIANS

1. All of the following factors contributed to the decline of the Plains Indians:

▶ The slaughter of 70 million buffalo

▶ The spread of epidemic diseases

▶ Construction of the railroads

B. PUBLICATION OF *CENTURY OF DISHONOR* (1881)

1. The book was written by Helen Hunt Jackson.

2. It aroused public awareness of the wrongs that the federal government had inflicted on Native Americans.

C. DAWES ACT OF 1887

1. The Dawes Act was a misguided attempt to reform the government's Native American policy.

2. The legislation's goal was to assimilate Native Americans into the mainstream of American life. It attempted to accomplish this goal by doing the following:

   ▶ Dissolving many tribes as legal entities

   ▶ Eliminating tribal ownership of land

   ▶ Granting 160 acres to individual family heads

D. CONSEQUENCES OF THE DAWES ACT

1. The Dawes Act ignored the inherent reliance of traditional Indian culture on tribally held land.

2. By 1900, Indians had lost 50 percent of the 156 million acres they had held just two decades earlier.

3. The forced-assimilation doctrine of the Dawes Act remained the cornerstone of the government's official Indian policy for nearly half a century.

4. The Indian Reorganization Act of 1934 (often called the Indian New Deal) partially reversed the individualistic approach of the Dawes Act by restoring the tribal basis of Indian life.

E. THE GHOST DANCE

1. The dance was a sacred ritual expressing a vision that the buffalo would return and all the elements of White civilization would disappear.

2. Fearing that the ceremony would trigger an uprising, the army attempted to stamp it out at the Battle of Wounded Knee.

3. As many as 200 Indian men, women, and children were killed in the Battle of Wounded Knee.

V. CONTRIBUTIONS DURING WORLD WAR II

A. THE HOME FRONT

1. Native Americans volunteered to work in defense industries.

B. THE NAVAJO CODE TALKERS

1. Fewer than thirty non-Navajos understood the Navajo's unwritten language.

2. Approximately 400 Navajos served as code talkers in the Pacific theater. Their primary job was to transmit vital battlefield information via telegraphs and radios in their native dialect.

3. The Navajo code talkers saved countless lives and played a key role in the battle of Iwo Jima.

KEY SUPREME COURT CASES AND TRIALS

1. The Marshall Court, 1801–1835

   ▸ John Marshall believed that the United States would be best served by concentrating power in a strong central government.

   ▸ Under Chief Justice John Marshall, Supreme Court decisions tended to promote business enterprise.

   ▸ Under John Marshall's leadership, the Supreme Court upheld the supremacy of federal legislation over state legislation.

2. *Marbury v. Madison*, 1803

   ▸ The case established the principle of judicial review.

   ▸ Judicial review gave the Supreme Court the authority to declare acts of Congress unconstitutional.

   ▸ *Marbury v. Madison* was one of a series of landmark decisions by Chief Justice John Marshall that strengthened the federal government.

3. *Dartmouth College v. Woodward*, 1819

   ▸ The Supreme Court ruled that the Constitution protected contracts from state encroachments.

   ▸ The ruling safeguarded business enterprises from interference by state governments.

4. *Worcester v. Georgia*, 1831

   ▸ The Supreme Court upheld the rights of the Cherokee tribe.

- President Jackson refused to recognize the Court's decision. He said, "John Marshall has made his decision: now let him enforce it."

- Because of Jackson's refusal to enforce the Supreme Court decision, the case was followed by the removal of the Cherokee from Georgia.

Test Tip

APUSH test writers expect you to be able to identify the Marshall Court and its key decisions. Remember, John Marshall was a judicial nationalist who opposed states' rights.

5. *Dred Scott v. Sandford*, 1857

- African Americans were not citizens and therefore could not petition the Court.

- Slaves could not be taken from their masters, regardless of a territory's "free" or "slave" status.

- This case was a major issue during the Lincoln–Douglas debates.

- The judge ruled that national legislation could not limit the spread of slavery in the territories.

- The *Dred Scott* decision invalidated the Northwest Ordinance and the 36°30' line in the Missouri Compromise.

- Here is an excerpt from the *Dred Scott v. Sandford* case:

   ". . . [T]he descendants of Africans who were imported into this country, and sold as slaves . . . are not included, and were not intended to be included, under the word 'citizens' in the Constitution, and can therefore claim none of the rights and privileges which that instrument provides for and secures to citizens of the United States."

- The Fourteenth Amendment invalidated the *Dred Scott* decision.

6. The 1873 Slaughterhouse Cases and the 1883 Civil Rights Cases

   ▸ These cases narrowed the meaning and effectiveness of the Fourteenth Amendment.

   ▸ These cases also weakened the protection given to African Americans under the Fourteenth Amendment.

7. *Plessy v. Ferguson*, 1896

   ▸ The case involved a dispute over the legality of segregated railroad cars in Louisiana.

   ▸ It upheld segregation by approving "separate but equal" accommodations for African Americans.

   ▸ It sanctioned "separate but equal" public facilities for African Americans.

8. Late Nineteenth- and Early Twentieth-Century Cases

   ▸ Supreme Court decisions strengthened the position of big business.

9. Sacco and Vanzetti Trial, 1920s

   ▸ The trial illustrated the widespread fear of radicals and recent immigrants.

10. The *Scopes* Trial, 1925

    ▸ The immediate issue was the legality of a Tennessee law prohibiting the teaching of the theory of evolution in the state's public schools.

    ▸ John T. Scopes was a Tennessee high school biology teacher who was indicted for teaching evolution.

    ▸ The Scopes trial illustrates the cultural conflict in the 1920s between fundamentalism and modernism.

11. *Korematsu v. United States*, 1944

    ▸ In early 1942, Japanese Americans living on the West Coast of the United States were forced from their homes into detention camps on the grounds that they were a potential threat to the security of the United States.

▸ The Supreme Court upheld the constitutionality of the relocation as a wartime necessity. Constitutional scholars now view the relocation as a flagrant violation of civil liberties.

12. The Warren Court, 1953–1969

▸ During a period of intense judicial activism, the Court used its power to promote social programs.

▸ The Warren Court reached notable and controversial decisions that established rights for those accused of crimes.

Test Tip

The Dred Scott case, Plessy v. Ferguson, *and* Brown v. Board of Education of Topeka *form a triumvirate of key civil rights cases. Be sure to study the key points about each case.*

13. *Brown v. Board of Education of Topeka*, 1954

▸ The ruling reversed the principle of "separate but equal" established in *Plessy v. Ferguson.*

▸ It declared racially segregated public schools inherently unequal.

▸ It declared that public school segregation is a denial of equal protection of the laws under the Fourteenth Amendment.

▸ This was the most important Supreme Court decision in the decade following World War II. It had widespread consequences for the rights of minority groups.

Test Tip

Remember, the Fourteenth Amendment guarantees citizens "equal protection of the laws." The Fourteenth Amendment is a key tool used by civil rights groups to overturn segregation.

14. *Baker v. Carr*, 1962

    ▶ The case established the principle of "one man, one vote."

    ▶ The Supreme Court required the reapportionment of districts for some state legislatures.

15. *Griswold v. Connecticut*, 1965

    ▶ The Supreme Court struck down a state law prohibiting the use of contraceptives.

    ▶ The Court proclaimed a "right to privacy" that soon provided the basis for decisions protecting women's abortion rights.

16. *Miranda v. Arizona,* 1966

    ▶ Controversial Warren Court decision establishing a defendant's Miranda rights.

    ▶ The Court ruled that no confession could be admissible unless a suspect had been made aware of his or her rights and the suspect had then waived those rights.

17. *Roe v. Wade*, 1973

    ▶ The U.S. Supreme Court upheld abortion rights for women.

    ▶ The Court based its decision, in part, on the right to privacy established in *Griswold v. Connecticut*.

KEY WORKS OF LITERATURE, ART, AND MUSIC

1. *Common Sense*, 1776

   ‣ This was a pamphlet written by Thomas Paine.

   ‣ It was a strongly worded call for independence from Great Britain.

   ‣ Paine opposed monarchy (he called King George a Pharaoh!) and strongly favored republican government.

   ‣ Paine offered a vigorous defense of republican principles.

   ‣ Paine helped overcome the loyalty many still felt for the monarchy and the mother country.

   ‣ Paine used biblical analogies and references to illustrate his arguments.

2. The Federalist Papers (*The Federalist*), 1787

   ‣ The Federalist Papers were written by Hamilton, Madison, and Jay to support ratification of the Constitution of 1787.

   ‣ They challenged the conventional political wisdom of the eighteenth century when they asserted that a large republic offered the best protection of minority rights.

3. *The Last of the Mohicans*, 1826

   ‣ It was written by James Fenimore Cooper.

   ‣ It was part of a series of novels known as the Leatherstocking Tales.

- Cooper was the first American writer to feature uniquely American characters.

- Cooper created the first genuine Western heroes in American literature.

- Cooper's novels gave expression to the concept of the "noble savage."

It is not a good use of your study time to memorize works of literature and their authors. You will not be asked to match a novel with its author. The authors are included here for easy reference. Instead, focus your studies on why the work of literature is important and what it illustrates about the time it was written.

4. *The Liberator*, 1831

- This newspaper was written and published by William Lloyd Garrison.

- It called for the "immediate and uncompensated emancipation of the slaves."

- Here is a famous quotation from The Liberator:

  "Let Southern oppressors tremble . . . I will be as harsh as Truth and as uncompromising as Justice . . . I am in earnest – I will not retreat a single inch—and I WILL BE HEARD!"

5. *Democracy in America*, 1835

- Alexis de Tocqueville was the author.

- He argued that American individualism arose as a result of the absence of an aristocracy.

6. The Hudson River School (mid-1800s)

- The Hudson River School was a group of artists led by Thomas Cole. These artists painted landscapes emphasizing America's natural beauty.

- The Hudson River School was America's first coherent school of art.

7. McGuffey Readers, 1836

   ▶ William Holmes McGuffey was the compiler and editor of these elementary school reading books.

   ▶ The best known and most widely used reading instruction books in the nineteenth century. It is estimated that during this time, four-fifths of all American schoolchildren used McGuffey Readers.

   ▶ The McGuffey Readers featured stories, poems, and essays supporting patriotism and moral values.

8. "Civil Disobedience: On the Duty of Civil Disobedience," 1849

   ▶ Henry David Thoreau was the author of this essay.

   ▶ He expressed opposition to the Mexican-American War.

   ▶ Thoreau argued that individuals have a moral responsibility to oppose unjust laws and unjust actions by governments.

   ▶ Thoreau's essay influenced Dr. Martin Luther King's philosophy of nonviolent civil disobedience.

9. *The Scarlet Letter*, 1850

   ▶ Nathaniel Hawthorne was the author.

   ▶ The novel dealt with the hypocritical legacy of Puritanism.

10. *Leaves of Grass*, 1855

    ▶ Walt Whitman was the author.

    ▶ Whitman's poems featured the Romantic movement's revolt against reason and the embrace of nature.

11. *Uncle Tom's Cabin*, 1852

    ▶ Written by Harriet Beecher Stowe, the novel strengthened Northern opposition to slavery.

    ▶ At the time, it was second only to the Bible in sales.

12. *Walden*, 1854

   ‣ Henry David Thoreau was the author.

   ‣ The novel espoused transcendentalism—that is, truth through inner reflection and exposure to nature.

   ‣ It recorded Thoreau's thoughts concerning the value of a life of simplicity and contemplation.

13. Horatio Alger Jr. Stories (1867–1899)

   ‣ Horatio Alger Jr. was the author.

   ‣ This is a collection of approximately 270 dime novels.

   ‣ Alger's novels feature rags-to-riches stories describing how down-and-out boys become rich and successful through hard work, honesty, and a little luck.

14. *A Century of Dishonor*, 1881

   ‣ Helen Hunt Jackson was the author.

   ‣ The book aroused public awareness of the federal government's long record of betraying and cheating Native Americans.

15. *The Influence of Sea Power upon History*, 1890

   ‣ Captain Alfred Mahan was the author.

   ‣ He argued that control of the sea was the key to world dominance.

   ‣ The book was very influential in promoting the growth of U.S. naval power during the late nineteenth century.

16. *How the Other Half Lives*, 1890

   ‣ Jacob Riis was the author.

   ‣ Riis was a journalist and photographer working primarily in New York City.

▶ Riis's book provided poignant pictures that put a human face on the poverty and despair experienced by immigrants living in New York City's Lower East Side.

17. "The Significance of the Frontier in American History," 1893

▶ Frederick Jackson Turner wrote this paper.

▶ He argued that the development of American individualism and democracy was shaped by the frontier experience.

▶ Turner's "frontier thesis" focused on the importance of the absence of a feudal aristocracy. In other words, the United States did not have a hereditary landed nobility.

▶ Here is a famous excerpt:

"From the beginning of the settlement of America, the frontier regions have exercised a steady influence toward democracy. . . . American democracy is fundamentally the outcome of the experience of the American people in dealing with the West. . . ."

18. *The Wonderful Wizard of Oz*, 1900

▶ L. Frank Baum was the author.

▶ *The Wonderful Wizard of Oz* was originally written as a political commentary on free silver and the plight of American farmers.

19. The Ashcan School of Art, early 1900s

▶ This was a group of eight American artists, led by John Sloan.

▶ Ashcan artists focused on depicting urban scenes such as crowded tenements and boisterous barrooms.

20. *The Jungle*, 1906

▶ Upton Sinclair was the author.

▸ The novel exposed appalling conditions in the Chicago meatpacking industry.

▸ It is a classic example of a muckraking novel.

▸ The novel helped bring about passage of the Pure Food and Drug Act and the Meat Inspection Act of 1906.

21. *Pragmatism*, 1907

▸ William James was the author.

▸ His concept of pragmatism held that truth was to be tested, above all, by the practical consequences of an idea, by action rather than theories.

▸ In short, beliefs should be tested by experience. The ultimate test of truth is experience, not logic.

▸ It is important to remember that William James and other pragmatists do not believe in the existence of absolute truth.

22. Lost Generation of the 1920s

▸ Key writers included Sinclair Lewis and F. Scott Fitzgerald.

▸ These writers were called the Lost Generation because they were disillusioned with American society during the 1920s.

▸ They criticized middle-class conformity and materialism. For example, Sinclair Lewis criticized middle-class life in novels such as *Babbitt* and *Main Street*.

23. Harlem Renaissance, 1920s

▸ Key writers included Langston Hughes, Zora Neale Hurston, Claude McKay, and James Weldon Johnson.

▸ They created distinctive African American literature.

▸ Writers expressed pride in their African American culture.

24. Jazz

    ‣ Black musicians such as Joseph (Joe) King Oliver, W. C. Handy, and Jelly Roll Morton helped create jazz.

    ‣ Jazz was especially popular among the youth because it symbolized a desire to break with tradition.

25. *The Grapes of Wrath*, 1939

    ‣ John Steinbeck was the author.

    ‣ Describes the plight of the so-called Okies who were forced to leave Dust Bowl-stricken Oklahoma in a futile attempt to find work in California.

26. *The Organization Man*, 1956

    ‣ W. H. Whyte was the author.

    ‣ The novel criticizes the homogenous culture of the 1950s.

    ‣ It criticizes American conformity and the belief that economic growth would solve all problems.

27. *On the Road*, 1957

    ‣ Jack Kerouac was the author.

    ‣ The novel expressed the alienation and disillusionment of the Beat Generation of the 1950s.

    ‣ Like other Beat Generation writers, Kerouac rejected middle-class conformity and materialism.

28. Rock 'n' Roll, 1950s

    ‣ Key musicians included Little Richard, Chuck Berry, and Elvis Presley.

    ‣ Rock 'n' roll first emerged during the 1950s.

    ‣ Rock 'n' roll was inspired and strongly influenced by black musical traditions, especially rhythm and blues.

29. *Silent Spring*, 1962

    ‣ Rachel Carson was the author.

▶ Her work protested the contamination of the air, land, and water with chemical insecticides such as DDT.

▶ The novel played a key role in sparking the environmental movement in the United States.

Rachel Carson and her watershed work **Silent Spring** *are important for the history of America's environmental movement. Rachel Carson was a woman of courage and conviction who alerted the public to the threat of chemical insecticides.* **Silent Spring** *aroused concerned Americans and helped launch the environmental movement.*

30. *The Other America,* 1962

▶ Michael Harrington was the author.

▶ It provided a poignant and influential report on poverty in the United States.

▶ The book played an important role in awakening President Kennedy's interest in the poor and showed the way for President Johnson's War on Poverty.

31. "Letter from Birmingham Jail," 1963

▶ The letter was written by Dr. Martin Luther King, Jr.

▶ Dr. King argued that citizens have "a moral responsibility to disobey unjust laws." Civil disobedience is thus a justified response to unjust laws.

KEY FACTS ABOUT LABOR UNIONS, LABOR LAWS, AND LABOR STRIKES

1. The Knights of Labor

   ▶ Under Terence V. Powderly's leadership, the Knights grew rapidly, peaking at 730,000 members in 1886.

   ▶ Membership in the Knights increased because of a combination of their open-membership policy, the continuing industrialization of the U.S. economy, and the growth of urban population.

   ▶ The Knights welcomed unskilled and semiskilled workers, including women, immigrants, and African Americans.

   ▶ The Knights were idealists who believed they could eliminate conflict between labor and management. Their goal was to create a cooperative society in which laborers, not capitalists, owned the industries in which they worked.

   ▶ The Haymarket Square riot in 1886 was unfairly blamed on the Knights. As a result, the public associated them with anarchists, and membership plummeted.

2. The Industrial Workers of the World

   ▶ The Industrial Workers of the World (IWW) was led by "Mother" Jones, Elizabeth Flynn, Big Bill Haywood, and Eugene Debs.

   ▶ Like the Knights of Labor, the IWW (or Wobblies) strove to unite all laborers, including unskilled workers and African Americans, who were excluded from craft unions.

- ▶ The IWW's motto was "An injury to one is an injury to all," and its goal was to create "One Big Union."

- ▶ Unlike the Knights, the IWW embraced the rhetoric of class conflict and endorsed violent tactics.

- ▶ IWW membership probably never exceeded 150,000 workers. The organization collapsed during World War I.

Eugene Debs ran for president several times and was one of the founders of the IWW. He was also one of the best-known socialist leaders in the United States. In a socialist system, the government owns the nation's basic industries and natural resources.

3. The American Federation of Labor

- ▶ The American Federation of Labor (AFL) was led by Samuel Gompers, the leader of the Cigar Makers Union.

- ▶ The AFL was an alliance of skilled workers in craft unions.

- ▶ Under Gompers's leadership, the AFL concentrated on bread-and-butter issues such as higher wages, shorter hours, and better working conditions.

4. The Great Railroad Strike, 1877

- ▶ Provoked by the Baltimore & Ohio Railroad's decision to cut wages for the second time in a year.

- ▶ Remembered as the first general strike in U.S. history.

- ▶ Paralyzed the nation's commerce for forty-five days.

- ▶ Forced governors in ten states to mobilize 60,000 militia troops to reopen rail traffic.

5. Sherman Antitrust Act, 1890

- ▶ The act forbade only unreasonable combinations or contracts in restraint of trade.

▶ It had little immediate impact on the regulation of large corporations; it was first used effectively by President Theodore Roosevelt in the Northern Securities case in 1902.

▶ During the last decade of the nineteenth century, the primary use of the act was to curb labor unions.

▶ The act declared illegal "every contract, combination in the form of trust, or otherwise, or conspiracy in restraint of trade among the several states."

6. Homestead Strike, 1892

▶ The strike began as a dispute between the Amalgamated Association of Iron and Steel Workers (the AA) and the Carnegie Steel Company.

▶ The AA refused to accept pay cuts and went on strike in Homestead, Pennsylvania.

▶ The strike ultimately culminated in a battle between strikers and private security guards hired by the company.

7. Pullman Strike, 1894

▶ During the late nineteenth century, the U.S. labor movement experienced a number of violent strikes. The two best-known strikes were the Homestead Strike (1892) and the Pullman Strike (1894).

▶ When the national economy fell into a depression, the Pullman Palace Car Company cut wages while maintaining rents and prices in a company town where 12,000 workers lived. This action precipitated the Pullman Strike.

▶ The Pullman Strike halted a substantial portion of U.S. railroad commerce.

▶ The strike ended when President Grover Cleveland ordered federal troops to Chicago, ostensibly to protect rail-carried mail but, in reality, to crush the strike.

KEY THEMES AND FACTS

8. Anthracite Coal Strike of 1902

   ‣ This was a strike by the United Mine Workers of America in the anthracite coal fields of eastern Pennsylvania.

   ‣ It was arbitrated with the active involvement of President Theodore Roosevelt.

   ‣ This strike marked the first time the federal government intervened in a labor dispute as a neutral arbitrator.

9. The Wagner Act of 1935

   ‣ The act is also known as the National Labor Relations Act.

   ‣ It is often called the Magna Carta of Labor because it ensured workers' rights to organize and bargain collectively.

   ‣ Passage of the act led to a dramatic increase in labor union membership.

10. The Congress of Industrial Organizations

   ‣ The Congress of Industrial Organizations (CIO) was led by John L. Lewis.

   ‣ The CIO organized unskilled and semiskilled factory workers in basic manufacturing industries such as steel and automobiles.

   ‣ Here is how John L. Lewis explained the goals and strategy of the CIO:

   "The productive methods and facilities of modern industry have been completely transformed. . . . Skilled artisans make up only a small proportion of the workers. Obviously the bargaining strength of employees under these conditions no longer rests in organizations of skilled craftsmen. It is dependent upon a national union representing all employees—whether skilled or unskilled, or whether working by brain or brawn—in each basic industry."

11. The Split Between the AFL and the CIO

   ▸ The American Federation of Labor (AFL) split apart at its national convention in 1935.

   ▸ A majority of AFL leaders refused to grant charters to new unions organized on an industry-wide basis.

   ▸ The AFL favored the organization of workers according to their skills and trades.

   ▸ The CIO favored the organization of all workers in a particular industry.

12. Taft-Hartley Act, 1947

   ▸ The primary purpose of the act was to curb the power of labor unions.

   ▸ Supporters of the Taft-Hartley Act believed the following:

      — *Unions were abusing their power.*

      — *Widespread strikes would endanger the nation's vital defense industries.*

      — *Some labor unions had been infiltrated by Communists.*

      — *Employers were being coerced into hiring union workers.*

   ▸ Organized labor opposed the Taft-Hartley Act.

Test Tip

Two key labor laws you should know for the APUSH exam: the Wagner Act and the Taft-Hartley Act. The former helped organized labor by guaranteeing the right to organize and form unions. The latter was intended to curb the power of labor unions.

KEY THEMES AND FACTS

13. United Farm Workers

▸ The workers were organized and led by César Chávez, Dolores Huerta, Philip Vera Cruz, and Larry Itliong.

▸ This was a union of farm workers.

▸ César Chávez is recognized as a significant civil rights leader.

KEY FACTS
ABOUT TWENTY
LEGISLATIVE ACTS

1. Navigation Acts, 1651

   ▸ The Navigation Acts put mercantilism into practice. Colonial products that could be shipped only to England were listed.

   ▸ The acts were designed to subordinate the colonial economy to that of the mother country.

Don't overlook the Navigation Acts and mercantilism. They are key elements in the increasing tension between Great Britain and the colonies.

2. Sugar Act, 1764

   ▸ The Sugar Act was the first law passed by Parliament to raise revenue for the British Crown.

   ▸ The Sugar Act was designed to tighten enforcement of English customs laws in America.

   ▸ Following bitter protests from the colonists, British officials lowered the duties.

3. Stamp Act, 1765

   ▸ The primary purpose was to raise revenue to support British troops stationed in America.

   ▸ Issue raised: Does Parliament have the right to tax the colonies without their consent?

▶ The act was repealed primarily because colonial boycotts of English goods were hurting British merchants. In response to this act, colonial leaders also formed the Stamp Act Congress. Although the boycotts had more influence than petitions from the Stamp Act Congress, colonial leaders learned an obvious but important lesson for the future: There was strength in numbers.

▶ The Stamp Act was important for the following reasons:

— *It revealed that many colonists believed they were entitled to all the rights and privileges of British subjects.*

— *The colonists demonstrated their willingness to use violence rather than legal means to frustrate British policy.*

— *The British maintained that the colonies had no right to independence from parliamentary authority.*

— *Patriot leaders claimed that the act denied them their British birthrights.*

4. Coercive Acts, 1774

▶ The Coercive Acts were the British response to the Boston Tea Party.

▶ They were widely known in the colonies as the Intolerable Acts.

▶ Parliament closed the port of Boston and drastically reduced the power of self-government in the Massachusetts colony.

▶ The Coercive Acts also provided for the quartering of troops in the colonists' barns and empty houses.

5. Kansas-Nebraska Act, 1854

▶ The Kansas-Nebraska Act repealed the Missouri Compromise of 1820, thus heightening the sectional crisis.

▸ It applied the principle of popular sovereignty to the territories.

▸ The act permitted the expansion of slavery beyond the Southern states.

▸ It sparked the formation of the Republican Party.

Test Tip

The Kansas-Nebraska Act was one of the most important acts in U.S. history. Be sure you know that it repealed the Missouri Compromise of 1820, applied the principle of popular sovereignty to the territories, and galvanized the formation of the Republican Party.

6. Homestead Act, 1862

▸ The Homestead Act permitted any citizen or prospective citizen to claim 160 acres of public land and to purchase it for a small fee after living on it for five years.

▸ The Homestead Act played a role in encouraging the settlement of the Western frontier.

7. Chinese Exclusion Act of 1882

▸ The Chinese Exclusion Act was the first law to exclude a group from the United States because of ethnic background.

▸ It prohibited the immigration of Chinese to the United States.

▸ The act was strongly supported by working-class Americans.

▸ It reflected anti-immigration sentiment in California.

8. Dawes Act, 1887

▸ The Dawes Act divided Native American tribal lands into individual holdings.

▸ The purpose was to assimilate American Indians into the mainstream of American culture.

▶ Reflecting the forced-civilization views of the reformers, the act dissolved many tribes as legal entities, wiped out tribal ownership of land, and set up individual Indian family heads with 160 acres.

9. Sherman Antitrust Act, 1890

▶ The Sherman Antitrust Act forbade unreasonable combinations or contracts in restraint of trade.

▶ It had little immediate impact on the regulation of large corporations.

▶ During the last decade of the nineteenth century, the primary use of the act was to curb labor unions.

▶ In 1902, President Theodore Roosevelt used this act to attack a J.P. Morgan–led trust named Northern Securities Co. This successful attack led to many other successful antitrust lawsuits by the federal government during the Progressive Era.

10. The Pure Food and Drug Act, 1906

▶ The act was an example of Progressive Era legislation.

▶ It was prompted by the public outrage unleashed by the publication of Upton Sinclair's novel *The Jungle*.

11. Federal Reserve Act of 1913

▶ The Federal Reserve Act created a central Federal Reserve Board whose members were appointed by the president.

▶ It established a national system of twelve district banks, which were coordinated by a Washington-based board of governors.

▶ The Federal Reserve System made currency and credit more elastic.

Test Tip

Actions of the Federal Reserve Board spark headlines and heated debate. Be certain you can identify the Federal Reserve Board.

12. National Origins Act, 1924

    ▸ The primary purpose of the National Origins Act was to restrict the flow of newcomers from southern and eastern Europe.

    ▸ It established immigrant quotas that discriminated against southern and eastern Europeans.

    ▸ This act was the primary reason for the decrease in the numbers of Europeans immigrating to the United States in the 1920s.

13. National Industrial Recovery Act, 1933

    ▸ The National Industrial Recovery Act (NIRA) sought to combat the Great Depression by fostering government–business cooperation.

    ▸ The act allowed businesses to regulate themselves through codes of fair competition.

    ▸ The NIA did not succeed. In fact, the NIRA and the Agricultural Adjustment Act (AAA) were declared unconstitutional in 1935 and 1936*, respectively. In contrast, President Franklin Roosevelt's Social Security Act proved to be much more enduring.

14. Neutrality Acts, 1930s

    ▸ The acts were expressions of a commitment to isolationism.

    ▸ During the 1930s, isolationists drew support for their position from Washington's Farewell Address.

15. Social Security Act, 1935

    ▸ The Social Security Act was part of the New Deal program of reforms.

    ▸ The act created a federal pension system funded by taxes on workers' wages and by an equivalent contribution by employers.

---

* The AAA's problematic method of generating subsidies was remedied with the Agricultural Adjustment Act of 1938.

▸ The aging of U.S. citizens since the 1970s is widely seen as threatening the long-term solvency of the Social Security system.

16. Wagner Act, 1935

▸ The Wagner Act is also known as the National Labor Relations Act of 1935.

▸ It is also known as the Magna Carta of Labor because it ensured workers the right to organize and bargain collectively.

▸ It led to a rapid rise in labor union membership.

17. Lend-Lease Act, 1941

▸ The purpose of the Lend-Lease Act was to provide military supplies to the Allies.

▸ The Lend-Lease program was used primarily to help Great Britain and the Soviet Union resist Nazi Germany.

18. Taft-Hartley Act, 1947

▸ The primary purpose of the Taft-Hartley Act was to curb the power of labor unions.

▸ Supporters of the Taft-Hartley Act believed that unions were abusing their powers and that widespread strikes would endanger national defense industries.

▸ Organized labor opposed the Taft-Hartley Act.

19. Federal Highway Act of 1956

▸ The act created the Interstate Highway System.

▸ Interstate highways played a key role in promoting suburban growth.

20. United States Immigration and Nationality Act of 1965

▸ The National Origins Acts of the 1920s severely restricted immigration into the United States.

▸ The United States Immigration and Nationality Act of 1965 abolished the national-origins quota system.

IMMIGRATION AND MIGRATION

I. THE COLONIAL PERIOD

A. THE PURITANS

1. The Puritans immigrated to New England in the 1630s for the following reasons:

    ▶ A desire to escape political repression

    ▶ A desire to find new economic opportunities and avoid an economic recession in England

    ▶ A desire to escape restrictions on their religious practices

2. The Puritans who immigrated to New England were part of what is known as the Great English Migration that included about 70,000 people moving to various locations outside England. Over twice as many Puritans immigrated to the West Indies compared to New England.

B. MIGRATION TO APPALACHIA

1. The Proclamation of 1763 set a boundary along the crest of the Appalachians beyond which the colonists could not cross. The ban was an ill-considered attempt to prevent costly conflicts with trans-Appalachian Indians.

2. As American Indians were defeated, Scotch-Irish, German, and English immigrants moved into Appalachia.

3. British colonists were principally motivated to settle west of the Appalachians by the low price and easy availability of land.

American settlers ignored the Proclamation of 1763, but it is an important part of colonial American history.

II. THE EARLY NINETEENTH CENTURY: 1800–1850

A. THE IRISH

1. Ireland supplied the largest number of immigrants to the United States during the first half of the nineteenth century.

2. The Irish fled the devastating effects of the potato famine.

3. Most Irish immigrants settled in urban cities along the Eastern seaboard.

4. Many Irish immigrants worked on canal and railroad construction projects.

B. THE GERMANS

1. Germany supplied the second largest number of immigrants to the United States during the first half of the nineteenth century.

2. Many Germans were fleeing political turmoil in their homeland.

C. THE KNOW-NOTHING PARTY

1. The Know-Nothings were America's first nativist political party.

2. The Know-Nothings directed their hostility against Catholic immigrants from Ireland and Germany.

THE LATE NINETEENTH AND EARLY TWENTIETH CENTURY: 1880–1924

A. EXODUSTERS

1. Exodusters were African Americans who fled the violence of the Reconstruction South in 1879 and 1880.

2. Most Exodusters migrated to Kansas.

B. THE NEW IMMIGRANTS

1. Prior to 1880, most immigrants to the United States came from the British Isles and Western Europe.

2. Beginning in the 1880s, a new wave of immigrants left Europe for the United States. The so-called New Immigrants came from small towns and villages in southern and eastern Europe. The majority immigrated from Italy, Russia, Poland, and Austria-Hungary.

3. The New Immigrants settled primarily in large cities in the Northeast and Midwest.

4. Very few New Immigrants settled in the South.

C. THE CHINESE EXCLUSION ACT OF 1882

1. This was the first law in U.S. history to exclude a group because of ethnic background.

2. The act prohibited the immigration of Chinese to the United States.

3. It was strongly supported by working-class Americans.

4. It reflected anti-immigration sentiment in California.

D. NATIVIST OPPOSITION TO THE NEW IMMIGRANTS

1. Nativists opposed the New Immigrants of the late nineteenth and early twentieth centuries for the following reasons:

   ▸ The New Immigrants practiced different religions.

▸ The New Immigrants had different languages and cultures.

▸ The New Immigrants were willing to work for lower wages than native-born workers.

▸ The New Immigrants were not familiar with the U.S. political system.

E. THE NATIONAL ORIGINS ACT

1. The primary purpose of the National Origins Act was to establish quotas to restrict the flow of newcomers from southern and eastern Europe. These quotas were the primary reason for the decrease in the numbers of Europeans immigrating to the United States in the 1920s.

2. The quotas favored immigration from northern and western Europe.

3. The number of Mexicans and Puerto Ricans immigrating to the United States increased because neither group was affected by the restrictive immigration acts of 1921 and 1924.

IV. THE GREAT MIGRATION (OF AFRICAN AMERICANS)

A. CAUSES

1. In 1915, the overwhelming majority of African Americans lived in the rural South. Jim Crow laws denied African Americans their rights as citizens and forced them to endure poverty and systematic discrimination.

2. Beginning with World War I, the wartime demand for labor attracted African Americans to cities in the North and West.

3. The black migration to the cities of the North and West continued during World War II.

V. IMMIGRATION FROM MEXICO

A. THE GREAT DEPRESSION

1. During the Great Depression, many Mexicans returned to their homeland.

B. SURGE IN MEXICAN IMMIGRATION

1. The following factors played an important role in Mexican immigration to the United States during the twentieth century:

   ▸ The relaxation of immigration quotas during the 1960s

   ▸ The desire to escape a crowded homeland with few economic opportunities

   ▸ The desire to take advantage of better job opportunities in the United States

   ▸ The desire to reunite with family members who had previously immigrated to the United States

 VI. POPULATION SHIFTS AFTER WORLD WAR II

A. FROM CITIES TO SUBURBS

1. The 1950s witnessed the beginning of a mass migration of middle-income Americans from cities to their surrounding suburbs.

2. The movement to the suburbs was facilitated by the construction of the interstate highway system.

B. FROM THE FROSTBELT TO THE SUNBELT

1. Beginning in the 1970s, the largest growth in population occurred in states below the 37th parallel, from Virginia to California.

2. The 1970s witnessed a significant migration of Americans from the Frostbelt (the North) to the Sunbelt (the South). This migration has continued to the present.

3. The South and West have experienced the greatest population gains since 1970.

C. FROM LATIN AMERICA AND ASIA TO THE UNITED STATES

1. The last twenty-five years have witnessed a significant increase in immigration from Latin America and Asia.

2. Latinos now make up nearly 33 percent of the population in Texas, Arizona, and California; they make up 40 percent of the population in New Mexico.

Test Tip

Most immigration questions on AP exams have focused on nineteenth- and early twentieth-century issues, but it is important to be familiar with more recent immigration issues as well.

KEY EVENTS IN U.S. FOREIGN POLICY: LATIN AMERICA

I. THE MONROE DOCTRINE

A. REASONS THE MONROE DOCTRINE WAS ISSUED

1. The Monroe Doctrine was intended to do the following:

   ▶ Warn France, Russia, and Spain against further colonization or intervention in the New World

   ▶ Express opposition to further European colonization in the New World

   ▶ Protect republican institutions of government in the New World

   ▶ Express America's intent to refrain from involvement in European rivalries

   ▶ Assert U.S. independence in foreign policy

B. PRINCIPLES OF THE MONROE DOCTRINE

1. The Monroe Doctrine was a unilateral declaration of the following principles:

   ▶ Europe and the Western Hemisphere have essentially different political systems.

   ▶ The American continents are no longer open to European colonization.

   ▶ The United States will regard European interference in the political affairs of the Western Hemisphere as hostile behavior.

> ▸ The United States will protect republican institutions of government in the Western Hemisphere.

> ▸ The United States will not interfere in the internal affairs of European nations.

C. ROLE OF THE BRITISH NAVY

1. The United States lacked the military power to enforce the Monroe Doctrine.

2. However, the principles expressed in the Monroe Doctrine were consistent with British foreign policy goals.

3. Although the British did not formally endorse the Monroe Doctrine, their navy was a de facto enforcer of its principles.

II. THE SPANISH-AMERICAN WAR

A. CAUSES OF THE WAR

1. The battleship USS *Maine* was sunk mysteriously in Havana harbor.

2. There was a circulation battle between the so-called yellow journalism newspapers of Joseph Pulitzer and William Randolph Hearst. The sensational stories in both newspapers played a significant role in arousing public support for a war to liberate Cuba from Spain and avenge the sinking of the *Maine*.

B. TERRITORIAL ACQUISITIONS

1. As a result of the Spanish-American War, Spain relinquished to the United States control of the following:

> ▸ Guam

> ▸ Puerto Rico

> ▸ Cuba

> ▸ The Philippines

2. When the United States established a protectorate over Cuba, it practiced imperialism.

C. THE DEBATE OVER ANNEXING THE PHILIPPINES

1. The Anti-Imperialist League opposed annexation, arguing that it violated America's long-established commitment to the principles of self-determination and anticolonialism.

2. Supporters of annexation argued that the United States had a moral responsibility to "civilize" the islands. They also pointed out that the Philippines could become a valuable trading partner.

III. THE ROOSEVELT COROLLARY TO THE MONROE DOCTRINE

A. REASONS THE ROOSEVELT COROLLARY WAS ISSUED

1. President Theodore Roosevelt worried that the Dominican Republic and other Latin American nations would default on debts owed to European banks. These defaults could then provoke European military intervention.

2. Roosevelt issued the Roosevelt Corollary to the Monroe Doctrine to forestall European intervention.

B. PRINCIPLES AND CONSEQUENCES OF THE COROLLARY

1. The Roosevelt Corollary asserted America's right to intervene in the affairs of Central America and the Caribbean.

2. It expanded America's role in Central America and the Caribbean.

3. It claimed America's right to act as an international police power in Central and South America. Presidents Roosevelt, Taft, and Wilson enforced the Roosevelt Corollary by sending U.S. troops to Cuba, Panama, Nicaragua, the Dominican Republic, Mexico, and Haiti.

4. Here is how Theodore Roosevelt explained and justified the Roosevelt Corollary:

"Chronic wrongdoing, or an impotence which results in a general loosening of the ties of civilized society, may in America, as elsewhere, ultimately require intervention by some civilized nation, and in the Western Hemisphere the adherence of the United States to the Monroe Doctrine may force the United States . . . to the exercise of an international police power."

Test Tip

The Monroe Doctrine and the Roosevelt Corollary are topics that have been tested frequently on the APUSH exam. Make sure that you carefully study this list of key points for both foreign policies.

IV. DOLLAR DIPLOMACY

A. REASONS FOR DOLLAR DIPLOMACY

1. During the presidency of William Howard Taft, U.S. policy in Latin America was primarily driven by concerns for U.S. economic and strategic interests in the region.

B. AN EXAMPLE OF DOLLAR DIPLOMACY

1. William Howard Taft's use of U.S. bankers to refinance the foreign debt of Nicaragua exemplifies dollar diplomacy.

V. THE GOOD NEIGHBOR POLICY

A. REASONS FOR THE GOOD NEIGHBOR POLICY

1. The United States sought greater cooperation with the nations of Latin America, primarily to develop a hemispheric common front against Fascism.

B. PRINCIPLES OF THE GOOD NEIGHBOR POLICY

1. Franklin D. Roosevelt's (FDR's) administration formally renounced U.S. armed intervention in the affairs of Latin America.

2. As part of its good neighbor policy, the United States participated in reciprocal trade agreements with nations in Latin America.

VI. THE ALLIANCE FOR PROGRESS

A. REASONS FOR THE ALLIANCE FOR PROGRESS

1. The Alliance for Progress was initiated by President John F. Kennedy (JFK) in 1961. It aimed to establish economic cooperation between North America and South America.

2. It was also intended to counter the emerging Communist threat from Cuba.

B. RESULTS OF THE ALLIANCE

1. The Alliance for Progress was a brief public relations success.

2. Although there were some limited economic gains, the Alliance for Progress was widely viewed as a failure.

3. The Organization of American States disbanded the Alliance for Progress in 1973.

Although most students are keenly aware of the Monroe Doctrine and the Roosevelt Corollary, few can identify FDR's good neighbor policy and JFK's Alliance for Progress. Both initiatives were short-lived and had few lasting consequences. Don't fall into the trap of neglecting these topics.

VII. KENNEDY AND CUBA

A. THE BAY OF PIGS

1. President Kennedy inherited from the Eisenhower administration a CIA-backed scheme to topple Fidel Castro from power by invading Cuba with anticommunist exiles.

2. When the invasion failed, Kennedy refused to rescue the insurgents, forcing them to surrender.

3. Widely denounced as a fiasco, the Bay of Pigs defeat damaged U.S. credibility.

4. The Bay of Pigs failure, along with continuing U.S. covert efforts to assassinate Castro, pushed the Cuban dictator into an even closer alliance with the Soviet Union.

5. Soviet Premier Khrushchev responded by secretly sending nuclear missiles to Cuba.

B. THE CUBAN MISSILE CRISIS

1. The Cuban missile crisis was precipitated by the discovery of Soviet missile sites in Cuba.

2. As part of the negotiations to end the Cuban missile crisis, President Kennedy promised to refrain from a military invasion of Cuba.

KEY EVENTS IN THE VIETNAM WAR

I. THE ROAD TO VIETNAM

A. POLICY OF CONTAINMENT

1. Following World War II, the United States adopted the policy of containment to halt the expansion of communist influence.

2. U.S. involvement in Vietnam grew out of the policy commitments and assumptions of containment.

B. THE FRENCH WITHDRAWAL

1. Following World War II, the French continued to exercise influence and control over Indochina.

2. The Viet Minh defeated the French at the pivotal Battle of Dien Bien Phu in 1954. Following their defeat, the French withdrew from Vietnam.

3. The United States refused to sign the Geneva Accords and soon replaced the French as the dominant Western power in Indochina.

C. THE DOMINO EFFECT

1. The United States believed that if one nation fell under communist control, nearby nations would also inevitably fall under communist influence.

2. Here is how then-Secretary of State Dean Rusk explained the domino effect:

> "If Indo-China were to fall and if its fall led to the loss of all of Southeast Asia, then the United States might eventually be forced back to Hawaii, as it was before the Second World War."

II. THE TONKIN GULF RESOLUTION, 1964

A. AN INCIDENT IN THE GULF OF TONKIN

1. The United States alleged that North Vietnamese torpedo boats launched an unprovoked attack against U.S. destroyers in the Gulf of Tonkin.

2. The facts of what actually happened have never been fully explained.

B. THE RESOLUTION

1. Congress responded to the unsubstantiated report of North Vietnamese aggression by overwhelmingly passing the Tonkin Gulf Resolution.

2. The resolution authorized President Lyndon Johnson to "take all necessary measures to repel any armed attack against the forces of the United States and to prevent further aggression."

3. The Tonkin Gulf Resolution gave President Johnson a blank check to escalate the war in Vietnam.

4. Within a short time, President Johnson began to increase the number of U.S. troops in Vietnam dramatically.

The Vietnam War was both long and complex. The Tonkin Gulf Resolution is a pivotal turning point that you absolutely, positively have to know. In essence, the resolution gave President Johnson a blank check to escalate the war.

III. THE TET OFFENSIVE, 1968

A. WHAT HAPPENED?

1. In late January 1968, the Viet Cong suddenly launched a series of attacks on twenty-seven key South Vietnamese cities, including the capital, Saigon.

2. The Viet Cong were eventually forced to retreat after suffering heavy losses.

B. CONSEQUENCES

1. The Tet Offensive undermined President Johnson's credibility.

2. As a result of the Tet Offensive, public support for the war decreased and antiwar sentiment increased.

3. Johnson withdrew from the 1968 presidential election race, throwing the race wide open. Republican candidate Richard Nixon won the election, thus ending the period of FDR-inspired liberalism (1932–1968).

IV. HAWKS AND DOVES

A. HAWKS AND THE SILENT MAJORITY

1. Hawks supported the Vietnam War.

2. The Silent Majority was the name given by President Nixon to the moderate, mainstream Americans who quietly supported his Vietnam War policies. Members of the Silent Majority believed that the United States was justified in supporting South Vietnam.

B. DOVES

1. Doves opposed the Vietnam War.

2. Senator William Fulbright was a leading dove. He wrote a critique of the war entitled *The Arrogance of Power*.

V. THE INVASION OF CAMBODIA AND PROTESTS AT KENT STATE, 1970

A. VIETNAMIZATION

1. Supported by the Silent Majority, Nixon began slowly to withdraw U.S. troops from Vietnam and replace them with newly trained South Vietnamese troops.

2. Known as Vietnamization, Nixon's policy promised to preserve U.S. goals and bring "peace with honor."

B. THE INVASION OF CAMBODIA

1. On April 29, 1970, President Nixon suddenly, and without consulting Congress, ordered U.S. forces to join with the South Vietnamese army in cleaning out the Viet Cong sanctuaries in officially neutral Cambodia.

2. Nixon defended the action, saying that it was necessary to protect U.S. forces and support Vietnamization.

C. KENT STATE

1. Angry students responded to the Cambodian invasion with demonstrations at campuses across the United States.

2. At Kent State University in Ohio, nervous members of the National Guard fired into a noisy crowd, killing four students and wounding many more.

Be sure you know about the invasion of Cambodia and the shootings at Kent State. Remember, the invasion of Cambodia was motivated by a desire to destroy Viet Cong sanctuaries in neutral Cambodia, thus protecting Nixon's policy of Vietnamization. The shootings at Kent State were an unexpected consequence of the Cambodian invasion.

VI. CONSEQUENCES OF THE VIETNAM WAR

A. THE WAR AND THE ECONOMY

1. The United States could not afford the massive costs associated with both President Johnson's Great Society programs and the Vietnam War.

2. Spending on both the war and social programs produced the high inflation rates of the late 1960s and early 1970s.

B. THE WAR AND INTERNATIONAL INVOLVEMENT

1. The Vietnam War increased public skepticism toward international involvement.

2. In 1973, Congress passed the War Powers Act, placing restrictions on a president's ability to wage wars.

PART IV:
TEST-TAKING STRATEGIES

STRATEGIES FOR THE MULTIPLE-CHOICE QUESTIONS

Your APUSH exam will begin with a fifty-five-minute section containing fifty-five multiple-choice questions. These questions will cover precontact Indian civilizations through recent years. The vast majority of the questions will cover the eighteenth, nineteenth, and twentieth centuries of U.S. history.

The score achieved on the multiple-choice section of the exam will be based on the number of questions answered correctly. Points are not deducted for incorrect answers or unanswered questions. Thus, there is no penalty for guessing. Don't waste precious time. If you do not have any idea how to answer a question, skip it and move on. If you can eliminate two or more answers, you should use the process of elimination and make an educated guess.

MULTIPLE-CHOICE STRATEGIES

The multiple-choice questions are vital to achieving a high score. Although they account for less than one-third of the APUSH exam's total time, they are worth 40 percent of the exam's total points.

The multiple-choice questions will all be based on a source document or graphic. This may be a primary source taken from the era in question or a secondary source, such as an historian's commentary on an issue, trend, or event. The graphics element might be a map, political cartoon, poster, painting, photograph, or chart. Each multiple-choice question will have four options: the correct choice and three distractors.

The multiple-choice section will not contain recall questions, in which you merely need to memorize facts, dates, or people. Instead, you will need to apply what you know about U.S. history to a question that requires analysis. Remember, however, that facts are the stuff of history and your mastery of them will contribute to your deeper understanding of questions, in both the multiple-choice section and the other sections of the exam.

When a set of questions is based on a graphic, such as a political cartoon, take time to make sure you understand the elements of the graphic. Read the question carefully. In many cases, the question's internal clues will help you decipher the right answer. And if you just don't know, mark the question to come back to later, and then guess. In such cases, you only lose by *not* guessing since no points are deducted for incorrect answers.

Here is a sample multiple-choice question and an explanation of the correct response:

> "Worst of any, however, were the fertilizer men, and those who served in the cooking rooms. These people could not be shown to the visitor—for the odor of a fertilizer man . . . who worked in tank rooms full of steam, . . . their peculiar trouble was that they fell into the vats; and when they were fished out, there was never enough of them left to be worth exhibiting . . ."

> Upton Sinclair, *The Jungle*, 1906

Which of the following features of the Progressive movement is directly related to the selection above?

    (A) *The Federal Trade Commission*

    (B) *Trust-busters*

    (C) *Muckrakers*

    (D) *Theodore Roosevelt's Square Deal*

The correct answer is (C) Muckrakers. Sinclair was one of the prominent investigative journalists who greatly influenced both U.S. public opinion and policy during the early years of the Progressive Era. While all of the other three options are related to Progressive Era issues, (C) is the correct answer.

Be sure to gauge your time so that you are able to answer all the questions. Try to leave some time to review your multiple-choice responses. For any you haven't yet answered, enter your best guess.

STRATEGIES FOR THE SHORT-ANSWER QUESTIONS

The short-answer questions are new for the 2015 AP U.S. History exam. There will be four questions, and you will have fifty minutes to answer them. A rectangular box is provided after each question, so your space is limited. These questions will address one or more of the thematic learning objectives and allow you to use a variety of examples from U.S. history to support your point. The thematic learning objectives are: identity; work, exchange, and technology; peopling; politics and power; America in the world; environment and geography; and ideas, beliefs, and cultures.

Each short-answer question will have three parts, and you will earn 0 or 1 point for each part. It is important to read the question carefully to make sure you are responding to what is asked. As with the multiple-choice questions, you will be asked to respond to a primary source, a historian's argument, or nontextual sources such as data or maps. In addition, you may be asked to consider a general proposition about U.S. history. You will need to identify and analyze examples of historical evidence in preparing all three parts of your response. Unlike the long essay and the document-based question (DBQ), you will *not* be asked to develop a thesis statement. Make your points as succinctly as possible and be specific in your response.

Here is a sample short-answer question:

Thomas Nast, *U.S. Library of Congress*

Using the 1874 cartoon above, answer each of the following questions:

a) What is the point of view of the cartoonist?

b) Provide an example of a failure of Reconstruction.

c) Provide an example of the impact of the Ku Klux Klan on African Americans in the South following the Civil War.

A good answer will identify the point of view that Thomas Nast espouses; that is, during the Reconstruction of the South, white groups, such as the Ku Klux Klan and the White League, worked together to return blacks to circumstances that were worse than slavery.

Your answer should also provide a specific example of one of the many failures of Reconstruction of the South, such as the institution of black codes limiting the civil rights of blacks. In addition, you will need to cite an example of the techniques used by the Ku Klux Klan as they restricted the social, economic, and political advancement of African Americans. For example, the Ku Klux Klan intimidated and terrorized blacks, particularly those who attained economic success.

Remember that you have only fifty minutes to answer all four questions. Be sure to leave yourself enough time to answer each question thoroughly.

Chapter 5

STRATEGIES FOR THE DOCUMENT-BASED QUESTION

After completing the multiple-choice and short-answer sections, you will have a well-deserved ten-minute break. When you return to your desk, your exam will resume with the document-based question (DBQ) essay. The DBQ is an essay question that requires you to interpret and analyze a set of seven primary-source documents. The documents typically include a graph, map, or political cartoon, as well as excerpts from diaries, speeches, and legislative acts.

The DBQ begins with a suggested fifteen-minute reading period. You should use this time to read the documents, organize your thoughts, determine a thesis, and prepare an outline for your essay. You will then have forty minutes to write your essay.

The DBQ causes many students a great deal of anxiety. The question is impossible to predict, and the documents are often taken from unfamiliar sources. Although the DBQ can be challenging, remember that the question always covers subjects described in the topical outline. The documents are brief and almost always easy to understand. You must use all or all but one of the documents in crafting your answer in order to get a good score.

PRACTICE MATERIALS

Practice is important to performing well on the DBQ. Practice will help you earn a high score. College Board materials are the best source of practice DBQs. Go to the AP United States History Course homepage at AP Central (*www.apcentral.collegeboard.com*) to find sample DBQs and actual student responses.

STRATEGIES FOR SUCCESS

Using authentic practice materials is as important as following a set of thoughtful test-taking strategies. Here is a guided set of strategies that can be used for the DBQ.

1. Carefully analyze the assignment.

   Begin your fifteen-minute suggested reading period by carefully examining the question. Sometimes students are so intent on telling everything they know about a topic or a historical period that they fail to read the question carefully.

2. Carefully read and analyze each document.

   Create an organizational chart or some type of graphic organizer. The documents will often have internal clues, such as a date or an author, that help you determine why it is included in the set. Depending on the type of question, your chart may include the author's point of view, position on an issue, or conflicting interpretations. Use your fifteen-minute reading period wisely to classify, interpret, and write notes about the documents.

3. Carefully write down outside information.

   Read the documents. Then pause and brainstorm potential outside information that you are reminded of by the documents. This is a crucial step. Remember, to obtain a high score, you will need to include outside information. Given the importance of outside information, it is vital that you organize your thoughts clearly and systematically.

4. Write a clear and responsive thesis that indicates your position on the question. If the prompt has multiple components, make sure your thesis addresses all parts of the prompt.

   Avoid generalities. Be as assertive and as specific as possible in stating your thesis in your opening paragraph. This is the most important paragraph you will write during the course of your exam, and your exam reader will focus on it when evaluating your entire essay.

5. Make sure the paragraphs following your opening thesis support your thesis in a logical way with specific examples.

    By the time students get to the document-based question, they are often fatigued and ready to be done with the exam. Some try to throw in every fact they know, whether each fact supports their thesis or not. Avoid this mistake and use your historical knowledge to craft an intelligent and accurate response that builds on the thesis in a step-by-step way.

The document-based question is the single biggest factor in determining your score on the exam. This one question counts for 25 percent of your total score. Give it your complete focus. Reread it before turning in the exam to make sure you have not made any technical errors.

STRATEGIES FOR THE LONG ESSAY

After completing your document-based question (DBQ), you may be aching for a break to rest your tired writing hand. Unfortunately, there is no break. Instead, you must press on and focus on the next and final APUSH challenge—the long essay.

You will have thirty-five minutes to complete your long essay, and you will choose one of two questions. Both questions will focus on the same historical thinking skill (i.e., causation, periodization, comparison, etc.), but the questions will ask about different time periods. The essay requires you to demonstrate your knowledge of a historical time period and to include specific and relevant historical evidence to support your thesis.

For more information about what is required for succeeding on the long essay, visit the College Board's AP United States History Course and Exam Description information at AP Central (*www.apcentral.collegeboard.org*). At this website, you will find examples of long essay questions and what the AP readers will look for when scoring the essays, as well as the rubrics that will be used for scoring.

STRATEGIES FOR SUCCESS

Using authentic practice materials is important, as is following good test-taking strategies. This section discusses strategies that will help you achieve high scores on your long essay.

1. Make pragmatic choices.

    Your first task is to select which of the two questions you want to write about. Above all, make a pragmatic, or practical, choice. Choose the topic you are best prepared to write about.

2. Write a clear, well-developed thesis.

Remember, a thesis statement is your position on the question. Writing a clear, well-developed thesis statement is essential to earning a high score. Make sure that your thesis addresses all parts of the prompt fully. Here is a clear, fully developed thesis statement and opening paragraph for a question concerning U.S. society in the 1950s:

> *Consensus and conformity dominated U.S. society during the 1950s. Americans lived in mass-produced suburbs where women returned to traditional gender roles and children watched homogenized television shows in which everyone looked alike. But not everyone in the United States liked Ike or loved Lucy. Led by Rosa Parks, Martin Luther King, Jr., and Thurgood Marshall, civil rights activists began to challenge Jim Crow segregation. At the same time, Beat writers such as Jack Kerouac questioned the value of middle-class conformity, and singers such as Little Richard and Elvis Presley pioneered a new and rebellious style of music called rock 'n' roll.*

3. Carefully write the rest of your essay.

Now that you have written a strong thesis as part of your opening paragraph, your final step is to finish your essay. As you write your essay, be sure to include specific, relevant, supporting historical evidence that supports your thesis.

4. Reread your essay to make sure that you have supported your thesis with accurate and specific examples and illustrations.

One common mistake students make is to answer with generalities. The exam readers will be reviewing the responses of thousands of students who have taken the exam. Make yours stand out by being accurate and specific.

INDEX

NOTES

NOTES

NOTES

NOTES

NOTES